EXTREME TEENS

Recent titles in
Libraries Unlimited Professional Guides for Young Adult Librarians
C. Allen Nichols and Mary Anne Nichols, Series Editors

Teen Library Events: A Month-by-Month Guide
Kirsten Edwards

Merchandising Library Materials to Young Adults
Mary Anne Nichols

Library Materials and Services for Teen Girls
Katie O'Dell

Serving Older Teens
Sheila B. Anderson

Thinking Outside the Book: Alternatives for Today's Teen Library
Collection
C. Allen Nichols

Serving Homeschooled Teens and Their Parents
Maureen T. Lerch and Janet Welch

Reaching Out to Religious Youth: A Guide to Services, Programs, and
Collections
L. Kay Carman

Classic Connections: Turning Teens on to Great Literature
Holly Koelling

Digital Inclusion, Teens, and Your Library: Exploring the Issues and
Acting on Them
Lesley S. J. Farmer

EXTREME TEENS

Library Services to Nontraditional Young Adults

Sheila B. Anderson

Libraries Unlimited Professional Guides
for Young Adult Librarians Series
C. Allen Nichols and Mary Anne Nichols, Series Editors

LIBRARIES
UNLIMITED
A Member of the Greenwood Publishing Group
Westport, Connecticut • London

Library of Congress Cataloging-in-Publication Data

Anderson, Sheila B.
 Extreme teens : library services to nontraditional young adults / Sheila B. Anderson.
   p. cm.—(Libraries Unlimited professional guides for young adult librarians, ISSN 1532–5571)
   Includes bibliographical references and index.
   ISBN 1–59158–170–2 (pbk. : alk. paper)
   1. Libraries and teenagers—United States. 2. Young adults' libraries—Activity programs—United States. 3. Young adults' libraries—Collection development—United States. 4 Teenagers—Books and reading—United States. 5. Young adult literature—Bibliography. I. Title. II. Series.
 Z718.5.A65 2005
 027.62'6'0973—dc22   2005016076

British Library Cataloguing in Publication Data is available.

Library of Congress Catalog Card Number: 2005016076
ISBN: 1–59158–170–2
ISSN: 1532–5571

First published in 2005

Libraries Unlimited, 88 Post Road West, Westport, CT 06881
A Member of the Greenwood Publishing Group, Inc.
www.lu.com

Printed in the United States of America

The paper used in this book complies with the
Permanent Paper Standard issued by the National
Information Standards Organization (Z39.48–1984).

10 9 8 7 6 5 4 3 2 1

To my parents, Ronald and Cheryl, who successfully raised
three somewhat extreme teens

CONTENTS

Series Foreword   xiii

Acknowledgments   xv

Introduction   xvii

1 What It Means to Be Extreme: Understanding
   Nontraditional Teens   1
      Who Is the Extreme Teen?   3
      Demographics of Extreme Teens   4
      Statistics about Extreme Teens   5
         Facts about Abortion   6
         Facts about Teen Pregnancy   6
         Facts about Dropouts   7
         High School Dropouts by Age, Race, and
         Hispanic Origin   7
         Juvenile Arrests for Selected Offenses, 2001   8
         Facts about Teen Mothers and Their Children   8
         Facts about Foster Care   9
            Extreme Teen Tidbits: People Who Were
            Nontraditional as Teens   9

Extreme Teen Tidbits: Books Made into Movies
about Extreme Teens   9
Extreme Teen Tidbits: Music about Extreme Teens   10
Extreme Teen Tidbits: Librarians Who Were
Extreme as Teens   10
Educational Situations   11
Unschooling   11
Resources about Unschooling   12
Homeschooling   13
Extreme Teen Tidbits: Reasons Why Teens Are
Schooled at Home   14
Resources about Homeschooling   14
Dual Enrollment   16
Extreme Teen Tidbits: Teens Involved in Dual
Enrollment   17
Dropouts   17
Extreme Teen Tidbits: Which Teens Drop Out of
High School   19
Resources about Dropouts   19
Literacy and Reluctant Readers   20
Resources about Literacy and Reluctant Readers   21
English as a Second Language and Immigrant Teens   22
Resources about ESL and Immigrant Teens   24
Living Situations   25
Homeless Teens and Runaways   26
Extreme Teen Tidbits: Reasons Teens Are
Runaways or Homeless   29
Resources about Homelessness and Runaways   30
Foster Care   30
Resources about Foster Care   31
Delinquency, Incarceration, and Violence   32
Resources about Incarceration, Delinquency, and
Violence   34
Emancipated and Independent Teens   37
Married and Cohabitating Teens   39
Sexual Activity   40
Resources about Sexuality   42
Pregnant and Parenting Teens   43
Resources about Pregnant and
Parenting Teens   44

Gay, Lesbian, Bisexual, Transgender, and
Questioning Teens   45
    Resources about GLBTQ Teens   47
Conclusion   48
Works Cited   49
For Further Reading   52

2 Outside the Mainstream: Service to Extreme Teens   55
Staff Selection   58
Staff Training   59
  In-house Training   59
  Library Organizations   60
  Conferences   61
Networking   62
Learning about Adolescent Stages   63
Special Considerations in Serving Extreme Teens   65
The Public Library Is Our Library:
Serving Homeschoolers   66
High School in the Morning and College in
the Evening: Serving Dual-Enrollment Students   66
For Those Who Did Not Stay in School:
Serving Dropouts   67
Can Johnny Read Yet? Literacy and Reluctant Readers   68
Is This Land Your Land? ESL and Immigrant Teens   70
It is a Big, Scary World Out There: Serving
Homeless and Runaway Teens   73
Busted: Serving Delinquent and Incarcerated Teens   75
  Helping Juvenile Delinquents   76
  Providing Outreach to Incarcerated Teens   79
    Extreme Teen Tidbits: I'm a Juvie Hall Junkie!   81
    Extreme Teen Tidbits: Responses from Teens at
    the Ocean County Juvenile Detention Center   82
    Extreme Teen Tidbits: A Glimpse Inside the
    Northeast Juvenile Detention Center in
    Fort Wayne, Indiana   82
    Extreme Teen Tidbits: How Juvenile Center
    Employees Responded When Asked, "What
    should librarians know about working with
    delinquent teens?"   83
Free at Last: Serving Emancipated Teens   83

With This Ring: Serving Married and
Cohabitating Teens   84
When the Condom (and the Water) Breaks:
Serving Pregnant and Parenting Teens   86
Not Just for the Birds and the Bees: Sexuality   88
Out and Proud: Serving Gay, Lesbian, Bisexual,
Transgender, and Questioning Teens   89
    Extreme Teen Tidbits: A Sampling of Library
    Web Pages Featuring Booklists for Gay, Lesbian,
    Bisexual, Transgender, and Questioning Teens   90
Conclusion   90
Works Cited   91
For Further Reading   92

3   Extreme Resources: Building Collections   95
    Determining Policies and Your Audience   96
        Words about Weeding   97
    Fiction   98
        Extreme Teen Tidbits: Chronology of Benchmark
        Novels about Nontraditional Teens   99
        Extreme Teen Tidbits: Insightful Quotations from
        Teen Literature   100
    Nonfiction   101
    Special Considerations in Providing Materials about
    GLBTQ Issues   102
        Dewey Know Dewey?   102
    Booklists, Pamphlets, and Magazines   103
    Beyond Books: Online Resources, Videos, DVDs,
    Audiobooks, and Software   103
    Suggested Resources   105
        Fiction about Incarceration   105
        Fiction about Violence and Delinquency   105
        Nonfiction about Delinquency, Incarceration,
        and Violence   107
        DVDs and Videos about Delinquency, Incarceration,
        and Violence   108
        Organizations and Online Resources about
        Delinquency, Incarceration, and Violence   108
        Fiction about Dropouts   109
        Fiction about Emancipated Teens   109

Nonfiction about Emancipated Teens 109
Fiction about Teens in Foster Care 109
Videos about Teens in Foster Care 110
Organizations and Online Resources about
Foster Care 110
Fiction about Married Teens 111
Fiction about Homelessness 111
Fiction about Runaways 112
Nonfiction about Homelessness and Runaways 113
Organizations and Online Resources about
Homelessness and Runaways 113
Videos about Homelessness 114
Nonfiction about Homeschooling 114
Fiction about ESL and Immigrant Teens 115
Nonfiction about ESL and Immigrant Teens 116
Organizations and Online Resources about ESL
and Immigrant Teens 117
Fiction about Pregnant and Parenting Teens 118
Nonfiction about Pregnant and Parenting Teens 119
Board Games for Pregnant and Parenting Teens 121
Organizations and Online Resources for Pregnant
and Parenting Teens 121
Fiction about Sexuality 124
Nonfiction about Sexuality 125
Organizations and Online Resources about Sexuality 125
Fiction about Same-sex Parents and Gay, Lesbian,
Bisexual, Transgender, and Questioning Teens 126
   General 126
   Bisexuality 127
   Gays 127
   Lesbians 128
   Same-sex Parents 129
   Transgender 129
Nonfiction for Gay, Lesbian, Bisexual, Transgender,
and Questioning Teens 129
   General 129
   Bisexuality 130
   Gays 130
   Lesbians 131
   Same-sex Parents 131

      Transgender   131
      DVDs and Videos about Same-sex Parents and
      GLBTQ Teens   131
      Organizations and Online Resources for
      GLBTQ Teens   132
    Conclusion   135
    Works Cited   135
    For Further Reading   135

**4 Beyond the Regular Routine: Promoting the Library
   and Resources**   137
    Promotion Assessment   138
      Promoting Programs   139
    A Sense of Place   140
      Extreme Teen Tidbits: Places to Promote
      Programs with Flyers   141
    Learning from Extreme Teens   143
    Networking in the Extreme Teen Community   144
    Administrative Support   146
    Do Not Just Talk, Booktalk   147
      Learning to Booktalk   148
      Extreme Teen Tidbits: Advice about Booktalking   150
      Sample Booktalks   151
        Booktalks about Delinquency, Incarceration, and
        Violence   152
        A Booktalk about Emancipated Teens   155
        A Booktalk about a Bisexual Teen   156
        Booktalks about Runaway Teens   156
        A Booktalk about Homeless Teens   157
        A Booktalk about Pregnant and Parenting Teens   158
    Conclusion   159
    Works Cited   159
    For Further Reading   159

Conclusion   163

Index   165

SERIES FOREWORD

We firmly believe in young adult library services and advocate for teens whenever we can. We are proud of our association with Libraries Unlimited and Greenwood Publishing Group and grateful for their acknowledgment of the need for additional resources for teen-serving librarians. We intend for this series to fill those needs, providing useful and practical handbooks for library staff. Readers will find some theory and philosophical musings, but for the most part, this series will focus on real-life library issues with answers and suggestions for front-line librarians.

Our passion for young adult librarian services continues to reach new peaks. As we travel to present workshops on the various facets of working with teens in public libraries, we are encouraged by the desire of librarians everywhere to learn what they can do in their libraries to make teens welcome. This is a positive sign since too often libraries choose to ignore this underserved group of patrons. We hope you find this series to be a useful tool in fostering your own enthusiasm for teens.

C. Allen Nichols
Mary Anne Nichols
Series Editors

ACKNOWLEDGMENTS

Thanks to Ricki Brown in Abilene, Texas, Marsha Grove in Champaign, Illinois, Rhonda Pinkney in Charlotte, North Carolina, and Jerry Thrasher in Fayetteville, North Carolina, for support and guidance when I was a young adult librarian at the Cumberland County Public Library & Information Center in Fayetteville, North Carolina. Also, thanks to my former staff in the Young Adults' Services Department at the Allen County Public Library in Fort Wayne, Indiana, for giving excellent service to extreme teens, and thanks to the library administration for providing the generous resources needed to enable that service. Last but not least, thanks to Zach Carter in Dover, Delaware, for his ongoing patience and sense of humor.

INTRODUCTION

> Not often does a high-school dropout and teen-age mother rise to high political office. Ruth Ann Minner, now a grandmother and lieutenant governor of Delaware, has made a life practice of breaking stereotypes. Minner, a Delaware native, left school when she was 16 to marry Frank Ingram.
>
> —Elaine Stuart, "From Dropout to Doer," *State Government News* 38, no. 1 (January 1995)

Governor Ruth Ann Minner of Delaware dropped out of school as a teenager to work on the family farm, married Frank Ingram, and became a teenage mother. After age thirty, she earned her GED. In 1993, she was given the "Delaware Mother of the Year" award. Governor Minner spent twenty-six years in elective office as a state representative, senator, and lieutenant governor.

Perhaps the extreme teens at your library will someday be governor of your state, which could lead to legislators in your state becoming financially supportive of libraries. In fiscal year 2005, state aid to public libraries in Delaware increased by $500,000. Considering that many libraries throughout the United States have had funding cuts recently, and keeping in mind that there are only three counties in Delaware, $500,000 is a generous overall increase.

Governor Minner is just one example of an extreme teen. As a high school dropout, a married teen, and a teen parent, she most likely faced some of the same difficulties as other extreme teens. So what is an extreme teen, and how do you know one when you see one? You probably will not recognize one when you see one, and that is part of the difficulty in serving this segment of the population.

For the purposes of this book, the words "extreme teen" do not merely refer to teens who are underserved or at risk, but it does include those teens. Typically, *underserved* populations are defined as those who are not properly served in some capacity. Some library committees serve specialized populations who are in the extreme category. The mission of the Outreach to Teens with Special Needs Committee of the Young Adult Library Services Association (YALSA) is to address the needs of teens who do not or cannot use the library because of socioeconomic, legal, educational, or physical factors.

Another example of extreme teens are *at-risk* youth. At-risk youth, typically, are those who are not likely to succeed in life as adults due to difficulties that they have had to face as children and teenagers. Experts in different fields may have varying definitions of what it means to be at risk. For instance, at the Annual Meeting of the American Educational Research Association in New Orleans, Louisiana, in 1988, Richard A. McCann and Susan Austin defined at-risk youth as students who are at risk of not achieving educational goals in order to become productive members of society, who exhibit behaviors that interfere with the education process, and whose community or family background may place them at risk (McCann and Austin, "At-Risk Youth: Definitions, Dimensions, and Relationships," Office of Educational Research and Improvement, Washington, DC, 1988). This practical definition of at-risk youth for educators may have some relevance to public librarians working with teens.

Extreme teens are those who are nontraditional in some way and who do not fit into the mainstream, for whatever reason, in your library service area. Keep in mind that extreme teens in one part of the United States may not be extreme in another. For example, in San Diego, California, where there are many bilingual students, teens who speak both English and Spanish may be considered mainstream, yet this may not be true in somewhere like rural Minnesota. Some parts of the country may have more high school dropouts while others may have more dual-enrollment students. Teen pregnancy is a widespread problem, yet some geographical locations may include an above-average number of teen parents. By being active in the community where you work, you can learn more about local demographics. This will help you better serve the various types of extreme teens in your service population.

There are many subgroups of extreme teens, but for the purposes of this book, the focus is primarily on teenagers who are extreme due to educational situations, living situations, and sexuality. Some of the most common and most extreme subgroups have been selected for coverage in this book. Other groups are not covered here because of space concerns. For example, this guide does not address the special needs of teens with physical or learning disabilities, developmentally disabled teens, and teens with a serious or terminal illness. Meeting the needs of these teens is certainly important, but requires specialized expertise and a level of detail that cannot be done in a volume of this size. The underlying message is diversity, however, and the overall lesson is to treat each person as an individual, regardless of the situation.

Some of the teens you encounter may fall into more than one subgroup of extreme teens, as Governor Minner did. A high school dropout may also be unable to read, and a student involved in dual enrollment may have been homeschooled since age five. It is not unheard of for a gay teen to be homeless, for many gay teens end up on the streets when their parents reject them. Likewise, many pregnant teens live on their own, especially if the male involved in the pregnancy is older and already living on his own.

Many librarians, like other adults, make assumptions that are counterproductive to teens who do not fit the mold. As our communities diversify, librarians must become sensitive to the needs of all individuals.

Extreme teens are probably in your community and using your library more than you realize. As a librarian, the first thing you must do is acknowledge the extreme teens in your community. Teens involved in educational situations outside of the mainstream qualify as extreme. Perhaps they have dropped out of school, have been homeschooled, or are enrolled in both high school and college. Teens whose living situations differ from that of most other teens can be considered extreme, whether they are homeless, runaways, living in a shelter or a group home, or even emancipated, meaning that they are living on their own and legally separated from their parents or guardians. Extreme teens are also teens who do not speak English or perhaps they cannot, or will not, read.

Some teenagers are married and live with their spouses. Involvement in situations relating to sexuality affects other teens. Some teens are sexually active, identifying themselves as straight, gay, bisexual, transgender, or questioning their sexual orientation. They may be pregnant, or they may already be parents.

Emancipated teens, who often need to make decisions affecting their health without parental involvement, qualify as extreme. Since laws regarding emancipation differ in each state, sometimes there are conflicts with this issue. For example, a seventeen-year-old who needs a certain treatment, but his parents are against medical assistance due to religious reasons, may have no say in the matter due to his age.

Whatever the circumstances surrounding teens who do not fit into the mainstream mold, it is important for you to realize that these teens need specialized programs and services by librarians who are caring and open-minded.

Mainstream young adult library services are underpinned with assumptions. For instance, most librarians serving teens schedule programs for after-school hours, assuming that teens are in school during the day. They also typically think that teens live with their parents. The information and programming needs of a teen living on her own and raising a child, or a teen who is homeless, or a gifted teen who attends college, are different than those of your typical middle or high school student. A homework center inside a public library is probably not going to be as important to the high school student who attends college in the evening. Day care services and parenting guidance might be more important to a young mother than a book club discussion of the Princess Diaries series. A teen who does not speak English may desperately need to know what community social services are available, while public library staff are offering programs on crafts or how to have a great prom night.

The library is often the only place for an extreme teen to find information and get support. Many teens use the Internet instead of relying on printed materials. Extreme teens may be less likely than other teens to ask librarians for help. Like others who have not been trained to conduct research, they may instantly conduct a Google search to find information. If you, as a librarian, take the time to reach out to extreme teens and promote library services, the lives and futures of these teens may improve. With ready-made handouts or Web links relating to homelessness, pregnancy, sexual identity, or homeschooling, your library staff will be better able to assist these specialized populations.

WHY SERVE EXTREME TEENS?

The American public library has historically been a place where anyone, regardless of race, gender, age, sexual identity, or socioeconomic status, has access to the information and resources that he or she needs to succeed in life. Unlike school libraries, where the collections typically reflect the curricular needs of students, public libraries strive to contain materials that reflect all interests and needs of the community. Also, unlike academic and special libraries, which cater to specific groups, public libraries provide information to people of all ages and from all walks of life. Public libraries are, therefore, a one-stop place for people who seek information about a variety of topics.

Teenagers crave information. They are at a point in their lives when they are leaving childhood behind and preparing for adulthood. As teens go through the normal stages of adolescent development, they need more information. Their cognitive abilities begin to sharpen as they age. They are exposed to new ideas and seek to learn about the ways of the world. It is natural, for example, for teens to have deep philosophical thoughts and to strive to get a grasp on who they are and where they are headed.

Extreme teens, who are not considered mainstream by the majority of society because of their societal circumstances, also seek information. Sometimes their needs are deadly serious, as in a homeless diabetic teen looking for health resources in the community. At other times, their information needs fall into the category of simple curiosity, such as trying to find out when their favorite rock star was born. Many extreme teens rely on the public library for information, especially if they are not enrolled in school. This segment of the population especially needs to interact with adults, such as librarians, who care about them and their future. They rely on library collections that support their needs.

Despite your own thoughts regarding extreme teens, it is your role as a librarian to serve them. The connections that you make with extreme teens may be within your library or outside the walls of your building. Perhaps you will reach an incarcerated teen who is inspired by one of your booktalks. Maybe the information about raising a child that you provided to a pregnant teen will help her be a better parent. A high school dropout who borrows a GED study guide from your library may thank you one day. You may grow as a person and feel a great sense of personal and professional satisfaction when helping an extreme teen whose life you may have just changed for the better.

ABOUT THIS BOOK

A wealth of excellent print and electronic resources are available to assist you in your role as a young adult librarian. Many professional resources view teens as a unified group; others concentrate on specialized services such as collection development, booktalks, teen spaces, and programming. Some books specifically address certain populations, such as at-risk teens, college-bound teens, homeschooled teens, and teen girls. In fields such as education, health care, social work, and criminal justice, books about serving nontraditional teens are plentiful. However, these resources provide little practical guidance for librarians to use with the exceptions to their teen populations.

Young adult service is not a "one size fits all" endeavor. The purpose of *Extreme Teens: Library Services to Nontraditional Young Adults* is to assist you in serving teens as unique individuals based on their special needs. The term "extreme teens" should not be considered derogatory. Instead, extreme teens are those who are different from most other teens because the lives they lead are different. This book cannot cover all cases of extreme teens, and there are many other types of situations and circumstances that could be explored, but the general principles set forth here can be applied to any teen.

Although teens typically experience difficulties as they grow into adulthood, some teens have unique situations that may help or hinder their teen experiences. This book is intended for young adult librarians, reference librarians, library administrators, and college librarians who may be serving nontraditional teens in some way. Youth service workers outside of the library science field, such as staff in prisons or nurses who work with pregnant teens, may find the book of interest as well. For example, the materials lists may be appropriate and useful. Staff at juvenile detention centers may be interested in the lists of books that portray incarcerated teens. Homeschoolers and their parents benefit from the suggestions of guides for creating a well-balanced curriculum.

Extreme Teens gathers concepts and practical tips from other, more focused resources, whether they are from the library science field or other specialized areas. Information from experts in various disciplines concerning youth services is supplemented with practical advice from librarians who have administered specialized programming and outreach for this part of the teen population. Social problems and situations are described and possible solutions proposed. So, for example, instead of merely explaining that teen homelessness is problematic and providing statistics, this book suggests how libraries may help homeless teens. In Chapter 1, "What It Means to Be Extreme: Understanding Nontraditional Teens," you will find national statistics on extreme teens and learn how to find out more about the specialized populations in your community. Various types of extreme teens are described, and their needs are discussed. You will also discover lists of resources, including books, journal articles, and some organizations that will be helpful in exploring more about extreme teens. In Chapter 2, "Outside the Mainstream: Service to Extreme Teens," you will learn how to select and train staff to be more sensitive to the needs of extreme teens. This chapter also includes information about programs and services that you may offer to extreme teens. Chapter 3, "Extreme Resources: Building Collections," includes information about the collection needs of extreme teens, including fiction, nonfiction, and electronic materials, along with an annotated bibliography of print and electronic works and a list of helpful organizations and Web sites. In Chapter 4, "Beyond the Regular Routine: Promoting the Library and Resources," you will find information about promoting the library, making the library a friendly place for extreme teens to visit, working with library administrators, and sample booktalks.

This book is not meant to be the final word on extreme teens, but it is intended to get you started. Use it as a guide to assist teens with special needs in your library. Use it to build new collections and to enhance existing ones, to spark ideas for programs, and to inspire fellow young adult librarians to work with their administrators to ensure that extreme teens are not overlooked in the public library. With your help, who knows what today's extreme teen may achieve tomorrow?

1

WHAT IT MEANS TO BE EXTREME: UNDERSTANDING NONTRADITIONAL TEENS

I'm not supposed to be here tonight. I'm on punishment. I'm supposed to be at the library.
—Elliot Goldberg, "Let's Meet for Marketing,"
Gloucester County Times (May 19, 1986): A-3

Wednesday is not just another day of the week. In high school my most extreme friend was named Wednesday. Maybe the inquiries about her unusual name contributed to her fully unique personality and sharp wit. Most people taunted her about her name. My family was no exception. Wednesday would call my house and if I was not home she would give the instructions, "Tell her to call Wednesday." My younger brother Brian would dryly respond, "Why wait until then?"

Wednesday and I were involved in many adventures together. The clerk at the used book store in our favorite shopping center kicked us out for throwing books. We were also told to leave Burger King after trying to smoke french fries that we had set on fire. Once we intentionally missed the bus and walked five miles to school, stopping at McDonald's, Dunkin' Donuts, a few convenience stores, and the hospital snack bar on the way.

When we arrived at our high school three hours later, the assistant principal was impressed but not terribly sympathetic.

Shop 'n' Bag, a grocery store, was the site of our greatest escapade. This was where Wednesday met Jimmy, who was nineteen and already out of high school. Shop 'n' Bag was having a singles night hosted by a radio station. I told the truth to my parents about where I was going, but as usual, Wednesday had to lie because she was being punished. In the produce aisle, a newspaper reporter interviewed her. She told him that she had lied to her parents: Her mother thought that she was at the library. He scribbled furiously. His article was in the newspaper the next day and included Wednesday's remark about pretending to be at the library. Luckily, my newspaper delivery route included her house, and we conspired so that I would refrain from delivering the paper to her doorstep that day.

When we were high school seniors, Wednesday became pregnant with Jimmy's baby. I suggested that they name the child Crouton if it were a boy or Rutabaga if it were a girl. They considered getting married in the produce aisle at Shop 'n' Bag. Wednesday attended our high school graduation, but she decided not to walk with her peers since she had a big belly. She concluded that the class of 1989 could walk without her and her fetus. Instead, she watched us from the bleachers.

Why did I acquaint you with wild stories about Wednesday, a pregnant teen? As a Young Adult Library Services Association (YALSA) Serving the Underserved (SUS) Trainer, I have learned about the power of empathy. Chances are, as a teen, you knew someone who was somewhat extreme. When training library staff, one especially useful exercise is to have the audience reminisce about their own teen years in order to empathize with teens who come to the library, or with teens in the grocery store.

After asking adults to remember their own teen years, memories typically begin flooding back. They remember the ups and downs of typical days as well as eventful moments such as the prom, driving for the first time, and graduating from high school. I usually ask the staff to complete a survey before training begins, and ask if they had any particularly good or bad experiences in libraries or with library staff members as a teen. We then talk about these experiences as a group. What I hope for in the training session is that audience members will learn from the mistakes or successes of librarians who had an influence on current library workers. Perhaps trainees will be inspired to have more patience and understanding when helping teens in libraries who may be shy, loud, rude, rushed, or, perhaps, pushing a baby stroller.

Adults, including librarians, often assume that teenagers typically fit into one type of cookie-cutter mold, that they are the gingerbread type who probably still live at home with their parents, who are still in middle school or high school, and who cannot wait to meet a member of the opposite sex, fall in love, get married, and have little gingerbread-like children. It is important that you try not to believe that all teens are the same, just as all librarians are not the same. When you attended your last library conference, did you play the game "spot the librarian" in the airport? Did you attempt to determine who was a librarian based on dress, actions, and words? If so, you were engaging in stereotyping. Although some aspects of each group of people in the world may be similar, it is dangerous to lump everyone into one category based on your own experiences. Teens have different types of living and educational situations, and also vary regarding their sexual activities and identities.

It is a fairly natural assumption that today's teens are the same as when you were a teen. This does not benefit teens, however, especially when they may be facing situations that you have never encountered or will never experience. For example, if you were born in the United States, it may be difficult for you to understand what it is like for immigrant teens who move to this country and have difficulty adjusting to new customs and a new culture. If you were one of the many people who attended college right after high school, and may have even gone right to graduate school after that, are you able to understand the needs of high school dropouts who are struggling to pass the GED? If you were a sexually abstinent teen, you might have difficulty being nonjudgmental toward pregnant teens.

WHO IS THE EXTREME TEEN?

Many teens are involved in situations that are not always considered mainstream. As with any circumstance, mainstream means different things to different people. In some parts of the country, for example, the number of teens learning English as a second language may be few and these teens may be considered nontraditional. In areas with many immigrants who have moved to the United States from other countries, teens learning English as a second language may be considered typical. Although many librarians assume that teenagers still attend high school, this is not always the case. Some teens are enrolled in college, some have opted to drop out of high school, and still others are homeschooled. Some teens are illiterate or severely below the educational levels of their peers.

Additionally, not all teenagers live in households that include a parent. Teens may be homeless, runaways, incarcerated, living alone, or residing in a group home. Some teens are already married and living with their spouses. Besides the typical stresses that burden teens, some teens have the responsibility of parenting their own child or children. Leading up to this situation, pregnant teens and teen males who are expectant fathers also have special concerns that deserve the attention of young adult librarians.

DEMOGRAPHICS OF EXTREME TEENS

Are extreme teens lurking in your library? They most likely are, but if not, they are certainly in your community. When you are working with extreme teens it is important that you understand the demographics relating to this specific segment of the population. Remember, though, it is not always easy to gather factual data about extreme teens. Just as teens responding to a questionnaire may not be honest about topics such as drug use or sexual activity, it may be difficult to gather other statistics about extreme teens. Although most demographics are based on states or the entire country, you can also gather data about teens in your community.

National statistics about extreme teens are available (e.g., *Statistical Abstracts of the United States: The National Data Book*), but it is even more important to learn about the extreme teens that exist in your local community. High schools, community colleges, and state departments of health and education may be able to provide you with information about high school dropouts, teens learning English as a second language, home-schooled teens, pregnant teens, parenting teens, and emancipated teens. It is generally more difficult to gather demographic information about teens who are runaways, homeless, or who identify themselves as gay, lesbian, bisexual, transgendered, or questioning (GLBTQ). To learn more about how many of these teens exist in your community and who would benefit from specialized library services, contact organizations serving these types of extreme teens.

Another way to connect with local teens and youth service providers is to conduct surveys. In addition to conducting surveys in the library, also consider doing them in other places where teenagers can be found, such as at schools, nearby youth organizations, and through agencies serving teens. Consider creating specialized surveys that may relate to extreme teens as well as comment cards that library patrons can complete, asking whether they found the information that they were looking for, whether staff members were friendly, and which sections of the library they visited. Some teens may be more likely to respond to surveys that are posted on Web sites instead of completing written surveys. Verbal, informal surveys can also be conducted simply by making sure that staff members ask extreme teens about their needs when they visit the library. It is important, however, that you are not confrontational in any way and that you do not ask for too much information.

Local statistics are generally available through city, county, and state governments. Some federal resources may also provide information about local demographics, such as the United States census. Many library facilities plans and other types of library-related studies may include information about local demographics as well, such as age, gender, ethnicity, socioeconomics, and levels of educational attainment. At the state level, some libraries engage in statewide planning for libraries, and consultants hired by state libraries may have also gathered useful demographic information that relates specifically to libraries. An example of this is the number of people in a specific geographic area who have used the library during a certain period of time. Using circulation statistics, it is also possible to determine the ages of those who are checking out library materials. Sometimes information about local groups and organizations are gathered by libraries and published in a printed format or on the library's Web page. Some community newspapers also gather and publish this information, as do some municipalities and state agencies.

Once you have gathered information about your local community, you can begin to determine the types of services or programs to provide to extreme teens. You will want to avoid duplication and try to partner with existing agencies as much as possible. If you are applying for grant funds to conduct any type of program, the people holding the purse strings are typically likely to award grant money to libraries that are working with other local agencies and organizations. Library administrators and library board members also like to see that librarians are taking advantage of existing local support for services to specialized populations.

STATISTICS ABOUT EXTREME TEENS

Here are some samples of national trends, but keep in mind that they may be more or less pertinent to some communities than others.

Facts about Abortion

- The United States accounts for approximately 3% of abortions worldwide.

- The majority of women (56%) are in their twenties. Fewer than 1% are younger than fifteen, while 19% are ages fifteen to nineteen. The abortion rate of teenagers has declined greatly in recent years due to the availability of long-acting hormonal contraceptives that can be injected.

- Women who have abortions are predominately young, single, and from minority and low-income groups.

- Almost 90% of abortions occur in the first trimester.

The Alan Guttmacher Institute and Physicians for Reproductive Choice and Health (PRCH), 2005, http://www.guttmacher.org/index.html.

Facts about Teen Pregnancy

- In 2001, the adolescent birth rate was 25 per 1,000 young women ages fifteen to seventeen. In this age category there were 145,324 births in 2001. The 2001 rate was a record low for the nation.

- The birth rate among adolescents ages fifteen to seventeen declined more than one-third, from 39 to 25 births per 1,000 between 1991 and 2001. This decline follows a one-fourth increase between 1986 and 1991. The 2001 rate was a record low for young adolescents.

- There are substantial racial and ethnic disparities in birth rates among adolescents ages fifteen to seventeen. In 2001, the birth rate for this age group was 10 per 1,000 for Asians/Pacific Islanders, 14 for White, non-Hispanics, 31 for American Indians/Alaska Natives, 45 for Black, non-Hispanics, and 53 for Hispanics.

Centers for Disease Control and Prevention, National Center for Health Statistics, 2001, http://childstats.gov/ac2003/indicators.asp?IID=132&id=4.

Facts about Dropouts

- Among youth ages sixteen to twenty-four, Hispanics accounted for 42% of all high school dropouts in 2002; however, they only make up 17% of the total youth population.
- Many youth who drop out of high school eventually earn a diploma or a GED. One study found that 63% of students who dropped out had earned a diploma or GED within eight years of the year they should have originally graduated.
- In 2002, males were more likely than females to be high school dropouts. In 2002, 12% of males ages sixteen to twenty-four were high school dropouts, compared with 9% of females. Although males make up one half of the population, they make up 57% of the dropouts in this age group.
- Foreign-born students had a dropout rate of 28% in 2002, compared with 18% for children born in the United States to foreign-born parents. While foreign-born students make up 12% of the total population of students in this age group, they make up 32% of the dropout population.

Child Trends Data Bank, 2002, http://childtrendsdatabank.org/indicators/1HighSchool Dropout.cfm.

High School Dropouts by Age, Race, and Hispanic Origin

Total dropouts in 2001

16-to-17-years-old	346,000
18-to-21-years-old	1,849,000

White

16-to-17-years-old	323,000
18-to-21-years-old	1,651,000

Black

16-to-17-years-old	55,000
18-to-21-years-old	331,000

Hispanic

16-to-17-years-old	113,000
18-to-21-years-old	823,000

Statistical Abstract of the United States: National Data Book, 2003, Washington: GPO, p. 177.

Juvenile Arrests for Selected Offenses, 2001

Violent crime	78,443,000
Weapons law violations	29,290,000
Drug abuse	146,758,000
Possession	122,109,000

Statistical Abstract of the United States: National Data Book, 2003, Washington: GPO, p. 209.

Facts about Teen Mothers and Their Children

- Teen mothers are less likely to complete high school (only one-third receive a high school diploma) and only 1.5% have a college degree by age thirty. Teen mothers are more likely to end up on welfare (nearly 80% of unmarried teen mothers end up on welfare).

- The children of teenage mothers have lower birth weights, are more likely to perform poorly in school, and are at greater risk for abuse and neglect.

- The sons of teen mothers are 13% more likely to end up in prison, while daughters of teen mothers are 22% more likely to become teen mothers themselves.

The National Campaign to Prevent Teen Pregnancy, February 2004, http://www.teen pregnancy.org.

Facts about Foster Care

- According to the 2001 Adoption and Foster Care Analysis and Reporting System Report, 160,419 people ages eleven to fifteen are in foster care and 89,632 people ages sixteen to eighteen are in foster care.
- Approximately 542,000 youth were in foster care as of September 30, 2001.
- Each year more than 20,000 youth age out of foster care.

Child Welfare League of America, December 27, 2004, http://www.cwla.org.

Extreme Teen Tidbits: People Who Were Nontraditional as Teens

Cameron Crowe: This movie producer dropped out of high school so that he could write about rock stars. He also wrote the book *Fast Times at Ridgemont High: A True Story* and the screenplay for the accompanying movie. Hey bud, let's party!

Whoopi Goldberg: This famous actress dropped out of high school, became addicted to heroin, and married her drug counselor—whom she later divorced.

Dr. Doogie Howser: Sure, he's a fictitious character in a television show, but it could happen! Doogie is a Princeton graduate and an M.D., all by age sixteen.

Gary Paulsen: A prolific writer for children and teens, Gary ran away from home at age fourteen and joined the carnival.

Extreme Teen Tidbits: Books Made into Movies about Extreme Teens

A Walk to Remember by Nicholas Sparks

Catch Me If You Can: The True Story of a Real Fake by Frank W. Abagnale and Stan Redding

Holes by Louis Sachar

Where the Heart Is by Billie Letts

Extreme Teen Tidbits: Music about Extreme Teens

"Runaway" by Bon Jovi

"She's a Little Runaway" by Rick Springfield

"The River" by Bruce Springsteen

"Young Turks" by Rod Stewart

Extreme Teen Tidbits: Librarians Who Were Extreme as Teens

1. "The fall of my junior year in high school, I found a book on the paperback rack at the public library. The cover showed a couple of well-built and well-endowed trapeze artists provocatively close to one another; it was clearly a gay romance. The same cover that attracted me caught the eye of the circulation clerk and she told me she didn't think she should check the book out to me, that it didn't even belong in the library." John P. Bradford

2. "I was academically gifted, and the public school system skipped me a total of two years. Therefore I entered high school at eleven, college at fifteen, and graduated at nineteen. I went to academic magnet public schools, and then to the University of Pennsylvania, an Ivy League school." Merry Luskin

3. "I was homeschooled from kindergarten until I began junior college, when I was seventeen. We were actually an 'unschooling' family, meaning that we never had structured class time, and very rarely used textbooks in any way. In our family, learning was as natural as breathing, and just as inevitable and unregulated." Brian Walton

4. "When I was sixteen I began the Running Start program in Washington State. I went to a local community college and took college courses for dual high school and college credit. During my junior and senior years I took only one course for one semester at the high school. I was completely separated from the high school and the teens who went to school there." Cheresse Thoeny

---

By now it is probably obvious that extreme teens are all around us, and deserve our attention and support. But before we explore how to do that, let us take a closer look at some of the ways in which teens are extreme.

EDUCATIONAL SITUATIONS

Forget about having to walk up a hill to school in the snow. Some teens are educated differently these days. Not all teens attend school. Just because someone is age sixteen does not mean that he or she is in high school. That person might be a high school dropout, already in college, homeschooled, or working toward a GED. Librarians need to be aware of alternative educational situations in order to serve extreme teens better.

Unschooling

I learned to mimic the opinions of teachers, and on command to vomit facts and interpretations of those facts gleaned from textbooks, whether I agreed with the facts or interpretations or not. (Derrick Jensen, *Walking on Water: Reading, Writing, and Revolution*, 2004, 4)

What is unschooling, and what do librarians need to know about this concept? My first exposure to the concept of unschooling was when I worked as the student liaison librarian at the Cumberland County Public Library & Information Center in Fayetteville, North Carolina. Eager to network with other librarians serving teens, I joined the young adult section of the North Carolina Library Association (NCLA). Our small but determined section of NCLA was a strong voice for young adult services. One way we spread information about our group was by producing *Grassroots: For High Risqué Librarians*, a newsletter that focused on young adult services available throughout the state while also highlighting national issues relating to young adult library services.

As a new recruit into the army of teen librarians, I found it beneficial to delve into past issues of the newsletter. I came across a blurb from Cindy Welch, former deputy executive director of YALSA and my predecessor as the student liaison librarian in Cumberland County. In the blurb, Cindy mentioned a book titled *The Teenage Liberation Handbook: How to Quit School and Get a Real Life and Education*, written by Grace Llewellyn (1991).

By including Llewellyn's work in my booktalk when I visited local schools, I felt as though I was able to directly reach teens who are like me and who may not enjoy learning in a classroom setting. Although I know the standard rules about booktalking, and that it is considered taboo to read directly from the books during booktalks, I typically read from page nine of the book because I found the following words to be so powerful:

> Did your guidance counselor ever tell you to consider quitting school? That you have other choices, quite beyond lifelong hamburger flipping or inner-city crack dealing?

After performing the booktalk, I asked the students why they thought that I told them about the book. The most common answer I got from them was that I wanted them to quit school. I explained that I was promoting the book because I was illustrating that the public library provides information about all types of topics, even books on how to learn outside of a classroom setting.

Unschooling is a movement somewhat related to homeschooling in which parents help their children and teenagers learn outside of a regular school setting. The integration of real life experiences is key in this process. For example, instead of learning about rocks by reading about them, students are encouraged to find rocks, examine them, and touch them. Also, in place of using headphones to listen to Spanish words, students are urged to talk with Spanish speakers and visit places where Spanish is spoken on a regular basis. Those who are involved in unschooling may rely heavily on the public library. These students may need information about travel, organizations, scholarships, and nontraditional education.

Resources about Unschooling

Falk, John H., and Lynn D. Dierking. 2002. **Lessons without Limit: How Free-Choice Learning Is Transforming Education**. Walnut Creek, CA: AltaMira Press. Like unschooling, free-choice learning is a movement involving learning as an experience that should be enjoyed rather than forced by any type of system or mandate. The book includes information about the free-choice learning movement, public education, and age-appropriate learning opportunities. One chapter in this book is devoted to adolescents. After explaining why the adolescent years are challenging, there is information about learning and teens in relation to independence, responsibility, and coming-of-age.

Jensen, Derrick. 2004. **Walking on Water: Reading, Writing, and Revolution**. White River Junction, VT: Chelsea Green. The work details the experiences of the author, who has taught writing in classrooms and maximum security prisons. It discusses the ways in which formal education has forced students to lose their creativity and conform to traditional thinking as defined by educators.

Llewellyn, Grace, and Amy Silver. 2001. **Guerilla Learning: How to Give Your Kids a Real Education With or Without School**. New York: Wiley. This work gives suggestions to parents for helping their teens and children learn through alternative methods in addition to school. It focuses on real world experiences as ways in which to learn about various topics instead of education in a traditional classroom setting.

Homeschooling

At home, labels like geek or nerd are rarely used. (Tamra Orr, *Violence in Our Schools: Halls of Hope, Halls of Fear*, 2003, 134)

Anyone working in a public library probably already knows that homeschoolers are regular library users, and typically, very supportive of public libraries. According to Jessica Garrison, author of "Staying Home to Go to School," published in the *Los Angeles Times* on May 8, 2001, "The latest believers in home schooling aren't the fundamentalist Christians or left-wing hippies of earlier days. Instead, the ranks of home schoolers are being swelled by a new wave of conventional parents who suspect that their children are being let down in some way by the public school."

Although in the past many homeschoolers have been elementary and middle school students, today more high school students are being schooled at home. Isabel Lyman, in a September 1, 1998, *USA Today Magazine* article titled "What's Behind the Growth in Homeschooling?" explores the lives of successful teens who have been homeschooled. Lyman wrote,

What type of young adults do homeschooling produce? Barnaby Marsh, who was homeschooled in the Alaskan wilderness, went on to graduate from Cornell University and was one of 32 Rhodes Scholars selected in 1996. Fifteen-year-old country singer LeeAnn Rimes skipped two grades as a result of homeschooling.

Extreme Teen Tidbits: Reasons Why Teens Are Schooled at Home

1. Some teens may have learning disabilities and may not be getting the type of assistance they need, while gifted teens may find that their high schools fail to challenge them or offer the appropriate academic courses that they need to prepare for college.

2. Teens in rural areas may find it is easier to be schooled at home due to the distance of the school building from home.

3. Some schools tend to focus more on athletics than academics, or give athletes more attention for their efforts, and students may believe that they would be better served in a different environment where the focus is on learning, not physical abilities.

4. Parents who cannot afford expensive private schools and do not have faith in public schools may believe that they can better educate their teens at home.

5. Teens and their parents may not agree with the religious ethics (or lack thereof) of the school.

6. Since bullying and violence may be commonplace in high schools, students may feel as though they are unsafe in a typical high school environment.

7. GLBTQ teens may feel more comfortable learning at home.

8. Teens may have been expelled from school or forced to leave for different reasons.

9. Families who move often determine that homeschooling is a better environment for their teens instead of having to change schools on a regular basis. This is particularly the case with military families and families with parents in occupations requiring frequent moves.

10. Teens who must move with their families during their junior or senior years in high school may decide that it is easier to learn at home instead of trying to meld into a new social and academic environment.

Resources about Homeschooling

Cohen, Cafi. 2000. **Homeschooling: The Teen Years**. New York: Prima Publishing. Gives practical tips to parents and teens on schooling at home.

Jones, Steve. 2000. **The Internet for Educators and Homeschoolers**. New York: ETC Publications. Explores the use of the Internet when schooling at home.

Lerch, Maureen T., and Janet Welch. 2004. **Serving Homeschooled Teens and Their Parents**. Westport, CT: Libraries Unlimited. Provides practical advice and a wealth of information to librarians about assisting homeschooled teens and their parents.

Lindsenbach, Sherri. 2003. **The Everything Homeschooling Book**. Avon, MA: Adams Media Corporation. Advises parents on teaching styles, types of homeschooling, how to get started, socialization, curriculums, schedules, record keeping, and more. A chapter on homeschooling in the teen years covers teaching high school courses, driver's education, social life, volunteering, working, preparing for college, and high school graduation. There is also a chapter which specifically focuses on college that discusses considering different types of colleges, entrance exams, and distance learning.

American Homeschool Association
PO Box 3142
Palmer, AK 99642
(907) 746-1336
AHAonline@aol.com
http://www.home-ed-press.com/AHA/aha.html
Supports the continued growth of the homeschooling movement by providing communications and networking for homeschooling families.

Homeschool Support Network
PO Box 708
Gray, ME 04039
(207) 657-2800
hsn@outrig.com
http://outrig.com/hsn/
Works to encourage parents who have chosen to educate their own children.

National Center for Home Education
PO Box 3000
Purcellville, VA 20134
(540) 338-7600
info@hsld.org
http://nche.hslda.org
Assists state homeschooling organizations by disseminating legislative information related to homeschooling.

National Home Education Research Institute
PO Box 13939
Salem, OR 97309
(503) 364-1490
mail@nheri.org
http://www.nheri.org
    The institute's mission is to produce high-quality research on home education, to serve as a clearinghouse of research for home educators and their supporters, and to educate the public about research findings related to home education.

Dual Enrollment

Each day, Jeremy Hoge bounds out of bed at 5:30 A.M. for an early band practice at Ritchfield High School near Minneapolis. Later, after advanced algebra, he dashes home for lunch. Then he grabs a different pile of textbooks and heads off to college. (Clayton 1999, 15)

By 1999, twenty-two states allowed students to enroll simultaneously in both high school and college. Legislators agreed that there are situations in which students without high school diplomas are suited to begin college courses. In twelve of these twenty-two states, the programs are so comprehensive that students pay little or no tuition. College and high school credits are earned at the same time. Some of these states allow eleventh and twelfth graders to take courses in which there are no comparable courses at their high schools.

During the summer months, many colleges and universities offer courses for high school students. Clayton writes that "Among the best known is the 'Talent Search' program at Johns Hopkins University in Baltimore, which is open to even younger prodigies. Typically, for-credit courses covering a year's worth of biology or chemistry or math are squeezed into a single three-week session" (1999, 15). At the University of North Texas and at the Texas Academy of Mathematics and Science, high school juniors and seniors study math and science, and when they graduate, they earn a high school diploma and credit for their first two years of college. In Santa Cruz, California, at-risk high school students were admitted into various colleges.

Extreme Teen Tidbits: Teens Involved in Dual Enrollment

1. Academically gifted teens who find college courses to be more challenging.
2. Teens who wish to get a jump-start on college courses.
3. Teens who are interested in a certain subject that is only taught on the college level.
4. Teens who are bored or disgusted with high school courses and culture.
5. Teens who feel more comfortable in college classes with more mature students.
6. Teens who move from one geographical area to another and find that they are more advanced in public school compared with where they moved from and are more at ease in college.
7. Teens who take college courses jointly with their parents.
8. Teens who intentionally drop out of school, obtain a GED, and begin college early.

Dropouts

I had been lonely in high school. From my seat in Biology, I had paid more attention to the weather reflected in the windows than to the frogs with their legs in the air. Wind blew germs across the classrooms. Plumbing sounded in the walls. Nickel-colored water dripped from a faucet. (Soto 1996, 2)

Jesse dropped out of high school in his senior year at age seventeen. He fled from his house and began living with his brother in an apartment near Fresno in order to escape from his alcoholic stepfather. He enrolled in the local community college where he adjusted well as a young college student, despite having to perform manual labor in the fields in order to pay his bills. He ate Ramen noodles and fruit that he stole from trees in his neighborhood.

Although the situation described is fictitious, the story is not unfamiliar. Soto is realistic in his portrayal of a teen who is nontraditional in that he has dropped out of high school, started college, and decided to live without his parents.

For various educational, financial, and cultural reasons, the high school graduation rate fluctuates across the United States and over time. According to an article by Patrik Jonsson published in the *Christian Science Monitor* in May 2001, many North Carolinians quit school due to new, more difficult requirements for graduation. In New York, students must past Regents exams before they can earn high school diplomas. In recent years, the high school dropout rate has increased because students have not been able to pass the exams. Also, more students are being held back. They may drop out because they are embarrassed to take classes with younger students. Some decide to leave high school and pursue a GED instead of a high school diploma.

In *Success without College: Why Your Child May Not Have to Go to College Right Now—and May Not Have to Go at All* by Linda Lee (2000), we are told that in the United States, almost half a million teenagers drop out of high school each year. Half of all freshmen in New York City schools will not graduate. Although Lee concedes that the number of high school dropouts is alarming, she adds that just because a person drops out of high school does not mean that their future cannot be bright. High school dropouts may become plumbers or computer programmers, and people working in these fields "earn a great deal more than most holders of a degree in European history" (p. 7). As an example, Lee describes a sixteen-year-old student, Cooper Small, who dropped out of school and began making $175 per hour as a computer programmer.

In El Paso, Texas, a project called Project Volver ("return" in Spanish), targets Hispanic Americans who have opted to drop out of high school. The program uses volunteers to track down students who have dropped out. A few weeks before the school year begins, the volunteers call the high school dropouts and urge them to re-enroll in school.

In Seattle, Washington, the Seattle School District has partnered with two community colleges in order to assist high school dropouts. Students are able to earn a GED, get career counseling, and earn a vocational certificate or associates degree. The state of Washington supports the program by paying for bus passes, GED exams, and textbooks.

Librarians serving high school dropouts should keep in mind that many opportunities exist for those who have decided not to continue in school. By learning about high school dropouts in your library's service area, you will be better equipped to serve this diverse population. High school dropouts may not always visit the public library on their own and may not be aware of the materials and services available.

Extreme Teen Tidbits: Which Teens Drop Out of High School

1. Teens who feel like social outcasts in a school environment where cliques are in command.
2. High school students who drop out of school in order to attend college or earn a GED.
3. Students who drop out due to economic reasons. For example, those who need to help out on a family farm or with a family business.
4. Teens from cultures or families that do not believe that a high school education is important for success. To students who expect they will inherit a farm or a business, attending high school may seem like a waste of time when they could be earning money.
5. Teens who must care for their children.
6. Teens who have younger siblings to care for during the day.
7. Teens with religious convictions that dictate other paths.
8. Teens with medical problems.
9. Teens who cannot meet the academic requirements required in high schools.
10. Teens who choose dropping out as an alternative to being kicked out.

Resources about Dropouts

Lehr, Camilla A., Ann T. Clapper, and Martha L. Thurlow. 2005. **Graduation for All: A Practical Guide to Decreasing School Dropout**. Thousand Oaks, CA: Corwin Press. This book for educators and school administrators provides advice for decreasing dropout rates and addressing the Adequate Yearly Progress requirement of the No Child Left Behind Act. Although it was not written for librarians, it will be useful to those serving dropouts who wish to learn more about the efforts to keep teens in the classroom.

National Research Council (U.S.) Committee on Educational Excellence and Testing Equity. 2001. **Understanding Dropouts: Statistics, Strategies, and High-Stakes Testing**. Washington, DC: National Academy Press. This work provides statistics about high school dropouts, explores tests and measurements used in the United States, and discusses equality and education.

Literacy and Reluctant Readers

We still have too many kids who are having difficulty with reading, especially in the middle and high schools. As a former middle and high school teacher, I had many students who had given up on reading. (MaryEllen Vogt, "Fitful Nights," *Reading Today*, December 2004/January 2005, 6)

When the National Endowment for the Arts (NEA) released a study of adults titled "Reading at Risk: A Survey of Literary Reading in America," there was a great deal of controversy about the results. The NEA study stated that the trend for adults is not to read literary works for pleasure and concluded that less than half of the adult American population reads literary works. In the *School Library Journal* article "The Truth about Reading" (November 2004), author Stephen Birkerts refers to the NEA study and discusses reading and youth. In the article he defends the role of technology in conjunction with reading.

Stephen Krashen, professor of education at the University of Southern California, reported that teenagers do like to read in the April/May 2001 issue of *Reading Today*. Literacy campaigns should ensure that teenagers have access to books. Although many middle class readers have ready access to books, potential teen readers may not be as likely to have books as readily available. Libraries, therefore, should focus on ensuring that materials are available for this age group.

Many librarians who work with teens will testify that many teens do like to read. However, as Krashen mentioned, it is important that librarians have well-stocked shelves of materials that are of interest to teenagers. Bookstore owners realize that the young adult market is massive. By visiting amazon.com or other online Web sites that sell books, it is quite easy to learn what teens are reading, what they enjoy, and what they would rather not read.

The International Reading Association, a strong advocate of literacy for all, has produced many useful tools for librarians and educators working with youth. Most significant is the association's document titled "Adolescent Literacy: A Position Statement," which provides guidelines to youth service workers. The document is available on their Web site at http://www.reading.org/resources/issues/positions_adolescent.html. Among other suggestions, the International Reading Association recommends that teens be provided with a wide variety of reading material and that they deserve "homes, communities, and a nation that will support their efforts to achieve advanced levels of literacy and provide the support necessary for them to succeed" (Jones 2002, 122).

It would be inaccurate to assume that all teens are able to read and write. Whereas much government funding is provided for childhood literacy up to the 3rd grade, adolescents in middle and secondary schools are too often sidelined. "The literacy development of a 12-year-old in middle school or a 17-year-old in high school remains as critical a concern to society as the literacy development of a preschool child or a child in the primary grades," writes Richard T. Vacca in "The Benign Neglect of Adolescent Literacy" (1997, 3). In the article, Vacca tells the story of one of his students who could not read well, remained working as an automobile mechanic, and who claimed that reading had robbed him of his manhood.

Another advocate for adolescent literacy is Donna Harrington-Leuker, a freelance education writer for the newspaper *USA Today*. In her article titled "Teens Need Literacy Lessons, Too" (2002), she explains why teens should be given attention when it comes to literacy. After the third grade, if a child cannot read, it is unlikely that he or she will ever learn to read. "Teens today live in a culture of audio and video, not print." She states that research indicates that high school students who read at the second- or third-grade level first need instruction in the relationship between sounds and spelling. Regarding President George W. Bush's administration and his plan for education reform, Harrington-Leuker gives sound advice to teen advocates: " 'Leave No Child Behind' was the administration's slogan for his education plan. In terms of reading, it's time to add a new riff on that: Leave no high school student behind."

Resources about Literacy and Reluctant Readers

Ammon, Bette, and Gale W. Sherman. 1999. **More Rip-Roaring Readers for Reluctant Teen Readers**. Englewood, CO: Libraries Unlimited. Provides librarians with information about books that may be appealing for reluctant teen readers and strategies for promoting these resources.

Aronson, Marc. 2001. **Exploding the Myths: The Truth about Teenagers and Reading**. Lanham, MD: Scarecrow Press. A collection of essays about teens and reading that features information about issues and trends related to young adult novels, publishers, realistic fiction, multiculturalism, and book awards.

Brozo, William G. 2002. **To Be a Boy, To Be a Reader: Engaging Teen and Pre-teen Boys in Active Literacy**. Newark, DE: International Reading Association. Assists teachers in reaching males who may dislike reading.

Irvin, Judith L., and James A. Rycik. 2001. **What Adolescents Deserve: A Commitment to Students' Literacy**. Newark, DE: International Reading Association. A guide for educators who are concerned about literacy and students.

Knowles, Elizabeth, and Martha Smith. 2001. **Reading Rules! Motivating Teens to Read**. Westport, CT: Libraries Unlimited. Provides an annotated list of professional resources and information about book clubs, booktalks, literature circles, information literacy, and young adult literacy.

Norton-Meier, Lori A. 2004. "The Bumper Sticker Curriculum: Learning from Words on the Backs of Cars." *Journal of Adolescent and Adult Literacy* 48, no. 3 (November): 260–263. The author describes her and her family's experiences as they learn by reading bumper stickers and also explains how bumper stickers can be used to enhance visual, critical, personal, and media literacy.

Reynolds, Marilyn. 2004. **I Won't Read and You Can't Make Me: Reaching Reluctant Teen Readers**. Portsmouth, NH: Heinemann. The author, who also writes fiction for teens, gives advice and personal anecdotal information about reaching teens who do not want to read. Contains URLs and books on various subjects that will appeal to teens with low literacy skills.

Sullivan, Edward T. 2002. **Reaching Reluctant Young Adult Readers: A Handbook for Librarians and Teachers**. Lanham, MD: Scarecrow Press. Discusses ways to approach teens who do not like to read and suggests book titles in different genres for them.

English as a Second Language and Immigrant Teens

> Per-Erik took a lot of grief after that. People stopped calling him by name and started referring to him as "the Swede," as if taking his name away made him a little less than human. That half the people in town had at least some Swedish or Norwegian blood didn't matter. (Carter 2004, 142)

In this story, Per-Erik Gustafs is a Swedish immigrant. He moves to the United States when his father is transferred after an American company in Green Bay, Wisconsin, is taken over by a Swedish company. Per-Erik has difficulty fitting in at school because some of his classmates' parents work for the company and they are not happy about the change in management. Although many people in the town are of the same ancestry as Per-Erik, he is still regarded as an outsider.

This collection of short stories gives an honest portrayal of what life is like for teen immigrants in the United States. Other cultural groups represented in the stories include Mexican, Venezuelan, Kazakh, Chinese, Romanian, Palestinian, Korean, Haitian, and Cambodian. In these stories, teens fight prejudice, overcome language barriers, and struggle with learning about their new culture while holding onto the past.

ESL teenagers typically have moved to the United States from other countries where they primarily spoke languages other than English. The number of ESL students in schools, especially public schools, has increased in recent years. In an article about what life is like for ESL students at J.E.B. Stuart High School in Falls Church, Virginia, author Joel L. Swerdlow reports that

> According to the 2000 census, 10 percent of America's 281 million residents were born in other countries, the highest percentage since 1930 and the largest number in U.S. history. (2001, 42)

At the high school, students are enrolled in special ESL classes, and the school is equipped with the necessary computer equipment, reading labs, and books to assist students.

In a 2002 report published by the National Clearinghouse for English Language Acquisition and Language Instruction Educational Programs in conjunction with the United States Department of Education and George Washington University, author Anneka L. Kinder states that during the 2000–2001 school year, approximately 1,424,329 students in grades seven through twelve in the United States are considered to be limited in their English proficiency. This number represents 6.9% of all students enrolled in school.

Oftentimes, immigrant teens may have more knowledge of the English language than their parents. These teens typically visit the library with their parents and communicate with the staff on behalf of their parents. It is sometimes difficult for these teens to take on adult roles at such young ages. They may be responsible for paying the bills, translating documents, and communicating with school officials in place of their parents.

You can help teens who may be frustrated by the English language by promoting the library and all of its resources, not just books. Teens can learn a lot from watching television and movies, especially about American customs and culture. Your recommendations in this area can be especially helpful, as immigrant and ESL teens may feel insecure in their new country and face discrimination in their daily lives. The public library can be a refuge for them as they seek information as well as acceptance.

Resources about ESL and Immigrant Teens

Brisk, Maria Estela, and Margaret M. Harrington. 2000. **Literacy and Bilingualism: A Handbook for All Teachers**. Mahwah, NJ: Lawrence Erlbaum Associates. Although the target audience for this book is teachers, it is useful for librarians who want to learn more about ESL teens. The first chapter defines literacy and bilingualism and the remaining chapters give practical suggestions to educators assisting students who are learning language skills.

Cushman, Kathleen, with the students of What Kids Can Do, Inc. Introduction by Lisa Delpit. 2003. **Fires in the Bathroom: Advice for Teachers from High School Students**. New York: The New Press. In Chapter 8, "Teaching Teenagers Who Are Still Learning English," teens from Korea, China, Brazil, Guatemala, and Mexico provide teachers with advice regarding how to work with a class full of high school students whose English is limited. There is a list of what students learning English wish teachers would ask, advice on building bridges between cultures, and classroom behavior issues.

Darby, Mary Ann, and Miki Pryne. 2002. **Hearing All the Voices: Multicultural Books for Adolescents**. Lanham, MD: Scarecrow Press. This work provides practical advice for using multicultural literature with teenagers and includes extensive annotated bibliographies on topics such as multiethnic families, nontraditional families, and so forth.

Hinton, KaaVonia, and Theodora Berry. 2004/2005. "Literacy, Literature, and Diversity." **Journal of Adolescent and Adult Literacy** 48, no. 4 (December/January): 284–288. The authors explore multicultural literature and its use in the classroom. They comment that students from various cultures, including African American, Cambodian, Chinese, and Indian, have said that it is valuable to read books about various cultures.

Luevano-Molina, Susan, ed. 2001. **Immigrant Politics and the Public Library**. Westport, CT: Greenwood Press. This collection of essays provides librarians with advice for serving immigrants in public libraries, especially in the creation of policies and procedures. For example, in "Passport to Promise: Public Libraries as Intellectual Spaces for Immigrant Students" (pp. 69–88),

JoAnn K. Aguirre discusses the importance of public library services for immigrant students along with facts about demographics and laws, such as Proposition 187 that deny unauthorized immigrants access to public services in California. A chapter by Evelyn Escatiola titled "Anti-Immigrant Literature: A Selected Bibliography," includes a list of resources pertaining to Asian, Caribbean, Mexican, and Latin American immigrants, laws, economics, education, women, and the environment.

McCaffery, Laura Hibbets. 1998. **Building an ESL Collection for Young Adults: A Bibliography of Recommended Fiction and Nonfiction for Schools and Public Libraries**. Westport, CT: Greenwood Press. This book includes an annotated, subject-specific list of five hundred works for ESL teens. Subjects include adventure, biographies, workplace, life skills, poetry, ethnic diversity, history, sports, and so on.

Moller, Sharon Chickering. 2001. **Library Service to Spanish Speaking Patrons: A Practical Guide**. Englewood, CO: Libraries Unlimited. After exploring the history of Spanish speakers, the author gives practical suggestions for serving library patrons based on age, including adults, children, and teens. There is also information about marketing the library to Latino teens, young adult literature, programming, and periodicals. One chapter is devoted to Internet sites for Spanish-speaking patrons, and appendices provide lists of selection tools, Listservs, organizations, book awards, book fairs, conferences, a translation of library-related terms, phrases in Spanish, the Dewey Decimal classification in Spanish, sample forms and surveys, and a list of publishers and distributors.

Pilger, Mary Anne. 2001. **Multicultural Projects Index: Things to Make and Do to Celebrate Festivals, Cultures, and Holidays Around the World**. Westport, CT: Libraries Unlimited. The author indexes thousands of books that include games, crafts, recipes, and activities relating to diverse cultures. This reference book may be useful to librarians who plan programs for immigrant teens.

Reid, Suzanne Elizabeth. 2002. **Book Bridges for ESL Students: Using Young Adult and Children's Literature to Teach ESL**. Lanham, MD: Scarecrow Press. Reid provides advice about teaching to ESL teachers, gives suggestions for teaching subjects such as history, math, and science, and includes a thorough bibliography of materials for children, teens, and librarians.

LIVING SITUATIONS

Move over, June Cleaver. You, too, Carol Brady. The traditional family of days gone by no longer exists in many households across the country. As a librarian serving teens, you need to realize that teens today come from all types of different backgrounds and living situations. Some live in cardboard boxes while others reside in castles on the hill. Whereas some teens have strict parents and a lot of rules, other teens already live on their own, or with their spouses, or are legally or illegally emancipated from their parents.

Homeless Teens and Runaways

The library was good. The dangerous kids won't show up there. Librarians are nice. (Carol Plum-Ucci, *What Happened to Lani Garver* 2002, 46–47)

In the 1930s, during the Great Depression in the United States, approximately 250,000 teenagers became homeless. Some teens rode the rails without having a ticket, and "They hopped on freight trains like fleas on a dog, in search of a job, a handout, or a place to sleep" (Schaumburg 2000, 18). Others became migrant farmers or worked on cattle ranches. President Franklin D. Roosevelt took steps to address the problem of homeless teens in 1932 by paying eighteen through twenty-five-year-olds $30 per month to work in the Civilian Conservation Corps. In 1935, high school students were given jobs as clerks, janitors, and gardeners after Congress established the National Youth Administration.

Not too much different from the 1930s, many teens today are runaways or homeless. "Today there are more homeless people in the United States than at any time since the Great Depression in the 1920s and '30s. Although being homeless is difficult for anyone, it is toughest on young people who may or may not be ready to be able to take care of themselves" (Parker 1995, 6).

To learn what it is like to be homeless, read some of the fine books that portray homeless and runaway teens. In the following excerpt from *Lucy Peale* by Colby Rodowsky, seventeen-year-old Lucy has recently run away from home. She uses the public library in Ocean City, Maryland, to learn about pregnancy and babies. Lucy is paranoid that the librarian knows she has been looking for information about being pregnant and that she has run away from home and sought refuge under the boardwalk. As Lucy explains,

I reckon she knows about the encyclopedia, about "Baby" and "Pregnant" and what I was looking to find out and how I'm not meant to be here and slept under the boardwalk and everything else besides. On account of this's a library and she's a librarian and maybe librarians *know* these things. (Rodowsky 1992, 40–41)

Sixteen-year-old Mary, portrayed in *Mary Wolf* (1995) by Cynthia D. Grant, is in a different type of homeless situation than Lucy Peale. Although she still lives with her parents, after Mary's father loses his job the family aimlessly travels around the country in an RV and stays in various trailer parks. Also by Grant, *The White Horse* (1998) tells the story of sixteen-year-old Raina as she battles with abuse, drugs, an unwanted pregnancy, and homelessness. Tar and Gemma, runaways in *Smack* (1998) by Melvin Burgess, also deal with drug addiction while living in a squat in England. *The Outsiders* (1967), a classic young adult novel by S. E. Hinton, portrays Ponyboy and Johnny, two teenagers who run away from home and live in a church after committing a crime.

Every day, thousands of homeless people, including teenagers, use libraries in the United States. To better assist the homeless teens and runaways in your library, get to know basic information about them. According to author Renee C. Rebman,

Runaways can be roughly classified into two groups, situational or chronic (or long-term). About 70 percent of situational runaways return home within one week, typically after two or three days. Another 14 percent return home within one month. Only about 5 percent stay away for a year or more. (2001, 8)

Although you may think of homeless people as living in larger cities, such as New York, Los Angeles, and San Francisco, homeless teens can be found in smaller cities. "When you think of Des Moines, you don't think of kids in the street. But they're there," comments Shane Stewart, a youth outreach worker in Des Moines, Iowa (Pierre 2002, A19). There are also homeless people in rural parts of the United States, and according to the National Coalition for the Homeless, there are very few homeless shelters in rural America. In these areas, the homeless are more likely to live with other family members (e.g., an emancipated sibling, uncle, or aunt) or friends, so it may seem as though there are fewer shelters when compared with larger cities (Vissing 1999).

Typically, the streets are not safe for homeless teens and runaways. Many resort to selling drugs and panhandling in order to stay alive. Often, both males and females become prostitutes. Teens are forced to grow up rather quickly when they live on the streets. Consider Alex Aborlleile, featured in a *New York Times* magazine article by Emily Nussbaum titled "His Only Address Was an E-Mail Account." Eighteen-year-old Alex left Philadelphia and headed for New York City with a few dollars, some oranges, and a backpack. Alex found his way to 42nd Street and Fifth Avenue.

> Since running away from home at 16, Alex had amassed more than 10 free e-mail accounts, with screen names like "ImpishBoi" and "ElusiveObserver." Within an hour, he was chatting with an N.Y.U. student, angling an invitation to his dorm room. He got it. That night, when the two of them traded sex for housing, it was a subtle hustle neither one acknowledged out loud. (2000, A81)

Homeless teens often live in different types of shelters depending on their situation. Emergency shelters are created in schools and churches when natural disasters occur; other shelters are more permanent for the chronically homeless. Life in shelters is often difficult for teens accustomed to living in a house. Their social lives change drastically. A homeless teen cannot bring friends to visit, and it is unlikely that he or she even has access to a telephone. It is usually difficult for teens to find a quiet place to study while living in a shelter. Thievery and losing personal belongings is common. When shelters are closed during the day, teens need a welcoming place to go until they reopen.

Although some teenagers stay in homeless shelters, others are placed into group homes, or in the care of government agencies, and sometimes are assigned to foster families. The Department of Children and Families (DCF) in Palm Beach, Florida, came under scrutiny in 2002 after a toddler and four teenagers went missing from custody. According to Kathleen Chapman ("Older Teen Runaways a Problem for DFC" 2002, 1B) it is difficult for DCF workers to find older teenagers who do not want to be found. Many of the children on the missing persons list are older teens who run away in order to avoid foster care. Although the streets are dangerous, group homes and homeless shelters are not always safe either. A study by the Hegeman Transitional Center, a safe haven for girls ages fifteen through eighteen in New York City run by the city's child welfare agency, found that the residents use drugs, drink, and sneak out for sex with neighborhood men. Personal items are stolen from residents, gangs beat up their enemies in the halls, residents are in possession of stolen cash and crack, rape is not uncommon, and girls are lured into prostitution.

**Extreme Teen Tidbits: Reasons Teens Are Runaways or
Homeless**

1. Teens usually run away from home in order to escape a negative family environment. Parents may be overly strict or punitive, or sexually abusive, physically violent, or addicted to drugs or alcohol.

2. Teens may be influenced to run away from home by peer groups, gangs, boyfriends, or girlfriends.

3. According to Barry Came, author of "Young, Gay—And Alone" (1993), the incidence of problems such as suicide, drug and alcohol abuse, and homelessness is higher among teenagers who believe they are or could be gay. Gay, lesbian, bisexual, transgender, and questioning teens may be forced to leave their homes because of parental disapproval, or they may feel as though they will be more accepted in a different environment, such as a large city where there is typically a community more accepting of their lifestyle.

4. Some homeless teens are called "throwaways" by advocates and outreach workers because their parents or other family members do not want them living at home anymore.

5. According to *Runaway Teens: A Hot Issue* by Renee C. Rebman (2001), most throwaways are older, about sixteen or seventeen years old. They are asked to leave home or are forced to do so because of their disruptive behavior. Leslie Forbes, executive director of Options House, a shelter in Hollywood, California says, "Sometimes we'll call the families, and they'll say, 'So you've got the little bastard? Well, you can keep him!'" (Hull 1994, 92).

6. Other teens may be part of an entire family that is homeless and living on the street, or in an abandoned building, automobile, hotel, or shelter.

7. Some families and teens may be homeless due to natural disasters or terrorist attacks. An article in the *Christian Science Monitor* (Marks 2001, 1) tells the story of Marion Legare who became homeless on September 11, 2001. "He was working as a contract hourly employee in a cafeteria on the 43rd floor of Tower 1 when the first plane hit the World Trade Center. He and his co-workers made it out, but when he went to his company to look for more work, there was none." After falling behind in paying his rent, Legare began living in a homeless shelter.

The kids that end up in group homes tend to be veterans of the foster care system, older teens who have bounced from placement to placement. They are among the most emotionally fragile children in the city's care. (Davis 1998, 19)

Resources about Homelessness and Runaways

Flowers, R. Barri. 2001. **Runaway Kids and Teenage Prostitution: America's Lost, Abandoned, and Sexually Exploited Children**. Westport, CT: Praeger Publishers. Examines the correlation between runaways and prostitution.

Holloway, John H. 2002/2003. "Addressing the Needs of Homeless Students." **Educational Leadership** 60, no. 4 (December/January): 89–90. Gives suggestions to educators about how to help students who face the challenges of high mobility, a difficult family life, and disrupted school attendance.

Hombs, Mary Ellen, ed. 2002. **American Homelessness, A Reference Handbook**. New York: ABC-CLIO. Covers the homeless problem through historical, biographical, and chronological presentations of facts, events, and statistics.

Hopper, Kim. 2003. **Reckoning with Homelessness** (Anthropology of Contemporary Issues series). Ithaca, NY: Cornell University Press. Details the history of homelessness, advocacy for the homeless in the United States, how people use airports as homes, and a study of homeless men. Although this work does not specifically focus on teenagers, the information provided may be useful for librarians who want to learn more about the subject.

Kusmer, Kenneth L. 2002. **Down and Out, on the Road: The Homeless in American History**. Oxford: Oxford University Press. This thorough resource provides historical information about homelessness in America.

Levinson, David. 2004. **Encyclopedia of Homelessness**. Thousand Oaks, CA: Sage Publications. This two-volume encyclopedia will be useful to librarians who wish to learn more about all aspects of homelessness, including its history, housing, social issues, health, street newspapers, and more.

Covenant House Nineline
(800) 999-9999
http://www.covenanthouse.org

Greyhound "Let's Find Them" Program
1-800-RUNAWAY
http://www.1800runaway.org

Foster Care

Adolescents placed in foster care are vulnerable and at risk of drug and alcohol abuse, pregnancy and sexually transmitted diseases, and suicide. (Bowman and Fike 1999, 144)

Teenagers in foster care are typically at risk because of their previous home situations, or they may become at risk as a result of being in foster care. These teens have special needs, like other extreme teens, because their social and educational lives have been disrupted. Teens in foster care may find that they need to switch schools regularly, making it difficult to keep up with academics. They may have difficulty making friends or they may decide not to bother, knowing that their home lives are unstable. Foster care may involve group homes or individual households where teens live with other families, and oftentimes, other foster teens and children.

Providing library services to teens in foster care may be difficult because of legal reasons. Foster parents or social service agencies may be reluctant to assume responsibility for library cards issued to minors. Since most libraries require the signature of parents or legal guardians before issuing library cards, teens in foster care may not be able to check out library materials or use library computers.

Resources about Foster Care

Blair, Julie. 2004. "Foster-Care Children Are Poorly Educated, 3-State Study Charges." *Education Week* 23, no. 24 (February 25): 12. This article presents the results of research about teens in foster care and concludes that these teens may face a bleak future because they lack strong academic backgrounds, have been expelled from school, or have had to repeat a grade.

Cameron, Theresa. 2002. **Foster Care Odyssey: A Black Girl's Story**. Jackson: University Press of Mississippi. This is the author's memoir. She was left with Catholic Charities in Buffalo, New York in the 1950s and spent her youth in foster homes.

Fisher, Antwone. 2004. **Someone There for Me: Everyday Heroes through the Eyes of Teens in Foster Care**. Washington, DC: Child Welfare League of America. This is a collection of stories written by youth about their experiences in foster care.

Kaufman, Leslie. 2002. "More of Those in Foster Care Are Teenagers, Report Says." **New York Times**, October 18, B2. Kaufman's article reports on the increasing percentage of teenagers in the foster care system.

Libal, Joyce. 2004. **A House between Homes: Youth in the Foster Care System**. Broomall, PA: Mason Crest. The first part of this book includes a fictional account of two youth in foster care; the second part gives information about the history of foster care.

Shirk, Martha, Gary Stangler, and Jimmy Carter. 2004. **On Their Own: What Happens to Kids When They Age Out of the Foster Care System?** Washington, DC: Child Welfare League of America; Boulder, CO: Westview Press. This work describes how teens cope when they turn eighteen and are no longer supported by the foster care system.

Toth, Jennifer. 1998. **Orphans of the Living: Stories of America's Children in Foster Care**. New York: Free Press. The author spent two years researching foster care systems and reports her findings in this book.

Delinquency, Incarceration, and Violence

But I volunteer down at the juvenile hall twice a week. I teach a writing class there. If you'd like to come down and visit sometime, the guys could tell you more than any books. (Salzman 2003, 10)

In *True Notebooks,* an Alex Award–winning book, Mark Salzman experiences an environment and lifestyle that books do not usually accurately describe, thereby providing a valuable service to juvenile delinquents. Although you can learn a lot about troubled teens by reading about them and watching movies and television shows about them, it does not compare with actually speaking and interacting with them. In conducting his research, Mark Salzman found that juvenile delinquents were able to write honestly about their lives. *True Notebooks* provides librarians with an authentic view of juvenile delinquents in Los Angeles.

In the 1800s, violent gangs of teenagers roamed the streets throughout the United States. During the early 1900s, juvenile delinquency steadily increased. The Federal Bureau of Investigation (FBI) determined that half of all the people arrested for motor vehicle thefts and arson in the early 1990s were under age eighteen. More than one hundred years ago the juvenile justice system was created based on the belief that young people are more likely than adults to be rehabilitated after committing a crime. Exploring the history of youth crime, Thomas Hine, author of *The Rise and Fall of the American Teenager,* comments that "The switchblades used by the juvenile delinquents who were so menacing during the 1950s were surely lethal, but an individual wasn't able to harm more than one person at a time. When young people have access to guns, a private dispute can turn into a massacre" (1999, 18).

In recent years, teenagers have begun committing crimes involving computers and the Internet. Aside from the longstanding stereotype of teen boys as computer hackers, both male and female teenagers have engaged in computer crimes other than hacking. Consider the three teenagers, two age eighteen and one age seventeen, in North Syracuse, New York, who attempted to blackmail a teacher for cash. These high school seniors posed as a twenty-three-year-old woman on the Internet to try to lure a teacher into engaging in cybersex. The students threatened to distribute copies of the e-mail messages unless the teacher paid them each $50, whereupon the teacher told school officials, according to the Associated Press. All three teens were charged with attempted grand larceny and coercion, all for the gain of a mere $50.

In Manassas, Virginia, a fifteen-year-old female went to the police with several copies of instant messages, claiming that other students had made threats against her and the school via America Online Instant Messaging. Ultimately it turned out that the fifteen-year-old had created fake screen names and engaged in chat sessions with herself, pretending to send threats to herself via other screen names for the purpose of getting other students into trouble. "Authorities characterized the episode as a high school dispute gone wrong and said it is an example of how the Internet has become a frequent source of crime for youngsters," said Josh White, author of *The Washington Post* February 6 (2001) article.

Do not be tempted to judge delinquents too quickly based on reports by the media. The phrase "If it bleeds, it leads" is timeless among journalists. The theory is that a bloody crime will surely make the front page of the newspaper and attract much attention. Many times, criminals are younger and may look quite innocent. Consider baby-faced Alex King, age thirteen, and his brother, Derek King, age fourteen. Both were found guilty in November 2002 of arson and second-degree murder after beating their father to death with a baseball bat. Both brothers, at the time of conviction, were of slight build and, when viewing media footage, had no trace of facial hair. Had the King brothers looked older, if they had been more robust looking with acne-ridden faces and mustaches, perhaps they would have received less attention from the media. The public might have viewed the King brothers as "regular" teenagers instead of young teenagers who looked a lot like children.

Murders are committed by teens, but not as often as most people are led to believe. Despite what the media tries to portray to the public, there are not millions of teens like Eric Harris and Dylan Klebold in the world, determined to massacre fellow students at their schools. "It's the rare teenager who commits murder, though it's certainly normal to think about it," comments Sabrina Solin Weill in *We're Not Monsters: Teens Speak Out about Teens in Trouble* (2002, 11).

Americans may be misinformed about youth crime. It is common for bad news to receive more attention than good news, and it is common for teenagers to be the focus of the bad news. It is not uncommon to come across screaming headlines that stereotype teenagers as evil.

Negative portrayals of teenagers by the media are not new.

In the 1944 *Liberty* magazine entitled "Youth Has Flamed Before," Edith M. Stern reassured her readers that the recent headlines about increases in juvenile delinquency were nothing new to America, citing complaints dating from 1770 about preventing couples from "irregular night walking, frolicking and keeping bad company," and from the 1870's about youths going on horseback rides unchaperoned. *Teenage Confidential: An Illustrated History of the American Teen.*

Today, teenagers are still misrepresented in the media. Statistics show that "Although youth homicides declined by 68% between 1993 and 1999, and are at their lowest rate since 1996, 62% of the public believes that youth crime is on the rise. While school-associated violent deaths have dropped 72% since 1992, and there was a less than one-in-three-million chance that a youth would be killed in a school last year, 71% of respondents to a *Wall Street Journal* poll thought a shooting was likely at their children's school," report Lori Dorfman and Vincent Schiraldi in "Judging from the News, You'd Think They Were a Plague" (*Los Angeles Times*, April 15, 2001, MZ).

Resources about Incarceration, Delinquency, and Violence

Angier, Naomi, and Katie O'Dell. 2000. "The Book Group Behind Bars." **Voice of Youth Advocates** (December): 331–333. Describes a book group for incarcerated youth and gives suggestions to librarians for replicating the program.

Association of Specialized and Cooperative Library Agencies. 1999. **Library Standards for Juvenile Correctional Facilities**. Chicago: American Library Association. Details standards for libraries in juvenile correctional facilities, including information about collections and policies.

Butts, J. A., and J. Buck. 2000. **Juvenile Justice Bulletin: Teen Courts—A Focus on Research**. Washington, DC: Office of Juvenile Justice and Delinquency Prevention. Reports on research related to teen courts.

Ferro, Jeffrey. 2003. **Juvenile Crime**. New York: Facts on File. Explores laws, the juvenile justice system, court cases, and provides readers with suggestions for researching juvenile crime. There is also an extensive glossary, a list of organizations and agencies, and statistics relating to trends in youth arrests.

Grisso, Thomas, and Robert G. Schwartz. 2000. **Youth on Trial: A Developmental Perspective on Juvenile Justice**. Chicago: University of Chicago Press. Experts in psychology and the law take a developmental perspective to answer whether youths have the maturity to participate as defendants in their trials in adult criminal courts and if they are as equally culpable as adults when they commit offenses.

Herald, Diana Tixier. 2004. "Making a Difference: Incarcerated Teens Speak." **Young Adult Library Services** 3, no. 1 (Fall): 20. The author describes her experiences in providing books to incarcerated youth.

Jones, Patrick. 2004. "Reaching Out to Young Adults in Jail." **Young Adult Library Services** 3, no. 1 (Fall): 16–19. Gives the results of research about public libraries providing outreach services to incarcerated youth.

Madenski, Melissa. 2001. "Books Behind Bars." **School Library Journal** 47, no. 7 (July): 40. Describes the experiences of librarian Naomi Angier who provided outreach services to incarcerated teens.

Maxym, Carol, and Leslie B. York. 2000. **Teens in Turmoil: A Path to Change for Parents, Adolescents, and Their Families**. New York: Viking. Although this book is geared for parents of teenagers, youth service workers will find it to be informative as well. After explaining society's concerns about teenagers, the authors present stories about five teenagers who are in turmoil. There is an extensive list of programs for additional help, such as alternative day programs, group homes, psychiatric hospitals, wilderness programs, religious outreach programs, ranch programs, and boot camps.

McCook, Kathleen de la Pena. 2004. "Public Libraries and People in Jail." **Reference and User Services Quarterly** 44, no. 1 (Fall): 26–30. Gives historical information about the ways that public libraries serve people in jail, explains how jail library services build communities, and highlights libraries in six different states that serve people in jail.

McShane, Marilyn D., and Frank P. Williams III, eds. 2003. **Encyclopedia of Juvenile Justice**. Thousand Oaks, CA: Sage Publications. This is a thorough encyclopedia that includes entries related to all aspects of the juvenile justice system, including delinquency theories, treatment, law, and public policy. Includes a comprehensive list of print and online resources for further information.

Mundowney, JoAnn G. 2001. **Hold Them in Your Heart: Successful Strategies for Library Services to At-Risk Teens**. New York: Neal-Schuman. Describes library programs throughout the United States that serve at-risk teens, including the San Francisco Bay Area Youth-at-Risk Project.

Polakow, Valerie, ed. 2000. **The Public Assault on America's Children: Poverty, Violence, and Juvenile Injustice**. Teaching for Social Justice series. New York: Teachers College Press. This work includes several essays that explore the link between poverty and violence, schools and zero-tolerance policies, the juvenile justice system, and throwaway children.

Rosenheim, Margaret K., ed. 2002. **Century of Juvenile Justice**. Chicago: University of Chicago Press. Details the history of juvenile justice in the United States.

Salzman, Mark. 2003. **True Notebooks**. New York: Knopf. The author spent a year teaching a writing class at Central Juvenile Hall in Los Angeles, and in this book, he chronicles his experiences with the students. Salzman's observations are interspersed with writings by the inmates, including reflections about their past crimes, feelings of anger, letters to their mothers, and what it is like to be in prison as a teenager. The author was involved with the Inside Out Writers Program, funded by the Alethos Foundation. The foundation funds professional writers who teach classes in detention centers and public schools throughout Southern California. This book was given YALSA's Alex Award as an adult book suitable for teens in 2004.

ABA Center on Children and the Law
http://abanet.org/child

Bureau of Justice Assistance
http://www.ojp.usdoj.gov/BJA

Center for Prevention of School Violence
1801 Mail Service Center
Raleigh, NC 27699
(800) 299-6054
http://www.ncdjjdp.org/cpsv/

Criminological Theory
http://www.crimetheory.com

Cybrary Criminal Justice Directory
http://talkjustice.com/cybrary.asp

Gang Crime Prevention Center
http://www.gcpc.state.il.us

Juvenile Justice Evaluation Center
http://www.jrsa.org/jjec/index.html

National Alliance for Safe Schools
PO Box 290
Slanesville, WV 25445
(888) 510-6500

National Campaign Against Youth Violence Headquarters
2115 Wisconsin Avenue, NW
6th Floor

Washington, DC 20036
(202) 366-6272

National Crime Prevention Council
1000 Connecticut Avenue NW
13th Floor
Washington, DC 20036
(202) 366-6272
http://www.ncpc.org/ncpc1.htm

National Criminal Justice Reference Service (NCJRS)
http://www.ncjrs.org

National Gang Crime Research Center
http://www.ngcrc.com

National School Safety Center
141 Dusenberg Drive
Suite 11
Westlake Village, CA 91362
(805) 373-9977

U.S. Department of Justice
http://www.usdoj.gov

Emancipated and Independent Teens

Three dollars may not sound like much, but that's almost a whole hour of work at Burger Boy. How much is the heat bill going to be? How much is the phone bill? What other bills am I going to have to pay? (Haddix 1997, 82)

In *Don't You Dare Read This, Mrs. Dunphrey* by Margaret Peterson Haddix, this fictional account of an emancipated teen describes what life is like for Tish, who tries to support her younger brother on her Burger Boy salary once both of her parents have abandoned her and her younger brother. You can better understand and empathize with teens in this situation by reading young adult literature.

Some teens are legally emancipated from their parents or caregivers. The term emancipation refers to a legal process by which a teen becomes independent from his or her parents or guardians. The age of emancipation varies in different states. In Connecticut, teens become eligible at age sixteen if they are (1) married, (2) in the U.S. armed forces, (3) living apart from their parents or guardian and managing their own money, or (4) if the court has decided that emancipation is in the best interests of the teen, his or her parents, or the teen's minor child.

Some teens may want to be emancipated from their parents because they are getting little assistance or support from them, especially financial support. Some determine that it is dangerous to live with their parents; others simply feel they can make it on their own before they reach age eighteen when they are no longer considered a minor in most states. Teens who live in group homes and foster care often become emancipated since their parents typically are not involved in their lives. Depending on state laws, some emancipated teens can live on their own, get medical care, enroll in school, buy property, get married, and join the military without parental permission.

Health issues are another great concern for some minors. For example, teens may seek abortions without parental consent, or, in some cases, parents may pressure them to seek an abortion when they do not want to have one. In some cases older teens have refused certain medical treatments because of religious or cultural reasons. Whether a minor was emancipated became a factor in the decision to provide treatment. Jehovah's Witnesses, for example, do not believe in blood transfusions. Some argue that older teens involved in Jehovah's Witnesses are not mature enough to make the decision to refuse a blood transfusion.

Regarding chronic illnesses, Stacy A. Teicher of the *Christian Science Monitor* writes, "A few judges have ruled in favor of teenagers who wanted to stop treatment that was expected to cure them but that had painful side effects. A 16-year-old boy from Massachusetts sparked a discussion of young patients' rights a few years ago when he temporarily ran away instead of facing continuing chemotherapy" (1999, 3).

In the state of New York, minors who are married, parents, or pregnant can make their own decisions regarding health care, just like adults. According to the New York Civil Liberties Union, organizations in New York will provide some minors with a letter of emancipation if health care workers question whether such care should be provided. Health care workers in other states consider the following factors before granting treatment to minors needing medical assistance: age, necessity of the treatment, and emotional and intellectual maturity. Teens in Massachusetts may become emancipated if they are pregnant or if they have a disease that poses a risk to public health, such as a sexually transmitted disease. In various states, some minors have become emancipated so that they have the right to sign themselves out of school when they are sick.

If parents pay their teens' medical bills, and if parents have access to insurance records, teens may not have much say in the confidentiality of their medical treatment, even if it concerns sensitive issues such as pregnancy, contraception, rape, suicide, drug and alcohol abuse, depression, or incest. Judy Foreman, writing for the *Boston Globe*, States, "But for many teenagers caught between childhood and adulthood, confidentiality can be elusive" (1999, D1). Oftentimes, teens will seek advice from doctors, not wanting to alarm their parents. Many teens also rely on online medical advice in the hopes that their questions will remain confidential.

Married and Cohabitating Teens

> I was sixteen, and Bo Jo was seventeen when we got married. As the statistics say, most teenagers who marry, marry because they have to. Or else. (Head 1967, 1)

Mr. and Mrs. Bo Jo Jones by Ann Head, is a classic young adult novel. It portrays a common stereotype of teenagers who must get married because a baby is on the way.

Throughout history, teen marriages have been portrayed in literature, music, and art. For example, Bruce Springsteen sings about a nineteen-year-old who marries his seventeen-year-old pregnant girlfriend, Mary, in "The River." His bleak description of the wedding involves going to the courthouse without flowers or a wedding dress. Long before Springsteen belted out sad tunes about the topic, teens married, and in some instances, at very young ages. During the Middle Ages, females as young as fourteen married. In 1947, the median age of marriage for women was 20.5, meaning that half of all brides were in their teens. "This dropped to 20.3 in 1950 and 20.1 in 1956, the all-time low for twentieth-century America, and well below the level in other developed nations at the time. In 1955 there were 1 million married teenagers, and in 1959 teenage pregnancy reached its modern-day peak" (Hine 1999, 234). In 1990 there were 598,000 married teens, and in 2000, 891,000 married teens. David Popenoe of the National Marriage Project at Rutgers University reasons that the increase is due to a trend toward conservatism among teens, welfare reform, less premarital sex, and fear of disease (*Washington Post*, November 9, 2002, A26).

Not all teens become married or live together because they are expecting a child; teens choose to become married for many reasons. Some are in love, like high school seniors Kevin Covington and Christie Keeley of Memphis, Tennessee, who were featured in *The Teen Appeal* newspaper, published monthly by the University of Memphis. "Kevin and Christie said they know they are perfect for each other and just didn't want to wait any longer to be together," writes Zakiya Larry. In *A Walk to Remember*, Nicholas Sparks writes about two teens—one is chronically ill—who are in love and decide to get married. In many high schools, it is not uncommon for teens to talk of wedding plans or to become engaged or "pre-engaged."

Immigration also has had a role in the increase in teen marriages. Many teens come to the United States from Latin America, sub-Saharan Africa, and Asia, where it is more common for the median age of a first marriage to be below age twenty. In one case, several teens in Orange County, California, got married in order to avoid being arrested. Former California governor Pete Wilson allocated eight million dollars toward a teen pregnancy prevention campaign to intensify statutory rape prosecutions in order to reduce welfare costs. State social service workers arranged marriages to prevent the fathers from being arrested for statutory rape.

Sexual Activity

The flirting process with Joey started at fifteen, and at sixteen I became sexually involved with him. How does someone that young and troubled handle a Joey Buttafuoco? I look back and shudder thinking how young I was. Sixteen. Do you remember when you were sixteen? (Fisher and Woliver 2004, 62)

It is natural to be curious about sex and quite common for many teens to engage in sexual experiences, but it is uncommon for teens to shoot the wives of their lovers, as in Fisher's case. In early adolescence, teens go through puberty and hormonal changes. Some young teens are sexually active while others wait before engaging in sexual activity. It is difficult to paint a true picture of teen sexuality because of the range of experiences, or lack thereof, and the ages at which these experiences occur. Some children, who are yet not teens, are sexually involved with other people, either willingly or forced. At the other end of the spectrum, some older teens and adults do not engage in sexual activity at all.

What do Amy Fisher, Soon-Yi Previn (Woody Allen's wife), and the late Nicole Brown Simpson all have in common? They were involved with adult males when they were still teens. This situation is not uncommon among teens. There is concern among youth advocates that adult males are impregnating teens. Many female teens choose older boyfriends because they are more mature (Shapiro 1995, 51–52). It is not unusual for high school juniors and seniors to date older males who may be in college or in the military. Older men may seek younger partners because they believe that there is less chance of acquiring a sexually transmitted disease. A lot of sex between adult males and female teens is not consensual and many female teens are the victims of rape by older men.

What do Sanjuanita Cardenas, Mary Kay Letourneau, and Tanya Hadden all have in common? These adults were sexually involved with minors. Cardenas, who slept with a fifteen-year-old, gave birth to his child. Letourneau began sleeping with Vili Fualaau when he was age twelve, and by August 2002 they had two children together. Letourneau and Fualaau finally married in 2005. Tanya Hadden, a California science teacher, had a sexual relationship with her fifteen-year-old student. Why did these women sleep with teens? "As crazy as it sounds, the women claim it was love—a love that transcended age difference and professional boundaries" (Dutton 2002, 134).

Some believe that adult men should know better while at the same time it is more socially acceptable for teen boys to sleep with adult females. "How about if an older woman provides a sexual initiation for a teenage boy? It's a fantasy dear to the hearts of many young men and a frequent theme of TV shows and movies, including the classic *Summer of '42*" (Peterson 2002, 1D). Others disagree with the fantasy concept, including boys who have been sexually abused by adult women. "Male victims of sexual abuse, while by far the minority, are speaking out more than ever. 'The number of reports that have been referred to us of women offending young males has grown by 60 percent in the past five years,' says Ilene Molinder, cofounder of Nichols and Molinder Assessments, which studies approximately 500 sex offenders a month nationwide" (Dutton 2002, 133). When considering sexual abuse of boys by older males, compared with the abuse of boys by older women, researchers state that "Abuse of boys by older males is reported more frequently than abuse by females, which suggests either that it is indeed more common, or that possibly sexual abuse of boys by females is more easily tolerated in general. Some respondents have stated that such a situation would have seemed more 'normal' to them" (Dorais 2002, 6).

Resources about Sexuality

Farrell, Sandie. 1997. "Sex: See Also 'Hornet's Nest'; We Can't Afford Not to Provide Books on Sex for Teens. **School Library Journal** 43 (June): 51. This article stresses that librarians need to provide information to teens about sex, despite the concerns of some parents and citizens groups.

Hickman, Tom. 1999. **The Sexual Century: How Private Passion Became a Public Obsession**. London: Carlton Books. This book details the history of sexuality in the media during the past century and is illustrated with color photographs from movies, television shows, and magazine covers.

Levine, Judith. 2002. **Harmful to Minors: The Perils of Protecting Children from Sex**. Minneapolis: University of Minnesota Press. The author discusses myths relating to sex, youth, and culture through headlines, interviews, and history.

MacRae, Cathi Dunn. 2004. "Young Adult Sexuality Research: How Do Teens Today Really Feel about Their Sexual Relationships—or Lack of Them?" **Voice of Youth Advocates** 26, no. 6 (February): 453. Explores statistics related to teens and sexuality.

Moran, Jeffrey P. 2000. **Teaching Sex: The Shaping of Adolescence in the 20th Century**. Cambridge, MA: Harvard University Press. Discusses the history of sexuality in relation to teenagers and how teenagers have been taught about sexuality.

Ponton, Lynn. 2000. **The Sex Lives of Teenagers: Revealing the Secret World of Adolescent Boys and Girls**. New York: Dutton. Written by a psychiatrist who works with troubled teens and their parents, this book covers the gamut of teen sexuality, including information about dating, puberty, masturbation, the relationship between sex and technology, sexual orientation, pregnancy, sexual abuse, and sexually transmitted diseases.

Tanenbaum, Leora. 1999. **Slut! Growing Up Female with a Bad Reputation**. New York: Seven Stories Press. Details the experiences of women ages fourteen through sixty-six who have been called sluts.

White, Emily. 2002. **Fast Girls: Teenage Tribes and the Myth of the Slut**. New York: Scribner. "Are you now or were you the slut of your high school class?" This author's query in a syndicated newspaper column, along with an 800 number, resulted in one hundred responses. The book covers high school culture, the slut archetype, and the attitudes of society toward sex, race, and popular culture.

Pregnant and Parenting Teens

DEAR ABBY: I think I am being discriminated against at my school because I'm 16, a sophomore, unmarried and pregnant. Because of my pregnancy, I'm getting into trouble because I'm missing school days to go to my doctor's appointments. (Dear Abby, November 27, 2002, http://www.uexpress.com/dearabby/?uc_full_date= 20021127)

This letter is one example of how pregnant teens are discriminated against by adults. In 1999, in Grant County, Kentucky, a federal judge ordered a National Honor Society chapter to admit two teenagers who were denied membership because they became pregnant through premarital sex. The committee that chose students for the National Honor Society considered premarital sexual activity when they determined the candidates' character. The pregnant teens claimed discrimination because other students who were accepted into the National Honor Society were not asked if they had engaged in premarital sex.

Many adults believe that pregnant teens are not likely to become successful even though many do lead productive lives. In "Not Your Average Teen Mom" (2000) Mary Guiden introduces Louisiana senator Paulette Irons, a mother at sixteen, who finished high school, law school, and ran for the state senate in 1995. "Teen Moms Who Beat the Odds" (DeWitt 1994, 53), published in *Essence,* is also useful for adults who question the future of teen parents. *You Look Too Young to Be a Mom: Teen Mothers Speak Out on Love, Learning and Success* (2004) edited by Deborah Davis, details how life changes for teen mothers once they have babies. Contributors discuss how they defied negative stereotypes, reached their goals, and relied on support from their families.

Not all teens faced with pregnancy are successful, though, and some even commit infanticide. In 1996, Amy Grossberg and Brian Peterson became so distraught that they killed their newborn in a motel in Newark, Delaware. The couple dumped the infant in a trash can immediately after his birth that November. This tragedy caused a stir throughout the state and even inspired a poem by Delaware poet laureate Fleda Brown (2002). "Amy and Brian" gives vivid details regarding the incident. In New Jersey in 1997, Melissa Drexler, age eighteen, gave birth in the restroom during her high school prom, left the infant in the trash can, and returned to the dance floor.

Public libraries should be places where pregnant teens feel comfortable to visit without the lack of confidentiality being a factor. Teens should be able to find reliable information in order to make decisions about their pregnancies, hopefully before occurrences of infanticide, risky self-births, or attempts at self-abortion.

Most attention on teen pregnancy has focused on females, and assistance is provided for mothers, but not always for fathers. "About 1 million teen-age girls become pregnant each year. More than half of them have babies. Ignoring the role teen-age boys play in this $6.9 billion public health problem makes no sense," writes Tim Wildmon in a *USA Today* (1998, 13A) article. Some teen fathers may become alienated from the female who is carrying their child. They may need both legal and financial information for ensuring parental rights.

Resources about Pregnant and Parenting Teens

Gross, Melissa. 1997. "Library Services to Pregnant Teens: How Can We Help?" **School Library Journal** (June) 43:36–37. Gives librarians practical advice in assisting pregnant teens including information about forming policies related to collection development.

Kaplan, Elaine Bell. 1999. **Not Our Kind of Girl: Unraveling the Myths of Black Teenage Motherhood**. Berkeley: University of California Press. Written by a sociologist who spent three years interviewing black teenage mothers and their mothers, this book explores race, class, and gender in relation to teen pregnancy.

Lipper, Joanna. 2003. **Growing Up Fast**. New York: Picador. Focuses on the lives of six teen mothers in Pittsfield, Massachusetts. After making a short documentary film about the teens, the author blended into their daily lives through the Teen Parent Program.

Allen Guttmacher Institute
120 Wall Street
New York, NY 10005
(202) 248-1111
info@agi-usa.org
http://www.agi-usa.org

Strives to provide accurate statistics and research about children and families and to educate the public on how social trends, such as teenage pregnancy, affect youth. Publishes several documents related to teen pregnancy including "Facts at a Glance," "Next Steps and Best Approaches to Preventing Adolescent Child-bearing," and "Welfare and Adolescent Sex: The Effects on Family History, Benefit Levels, and Community Context."

National Campaign to Prevent Teen Pregnancy
1776 Massachusetts Avenue NQ
Suite 200
Washington, DC 20036
(202) 478-8500
http://www.teenpregnancy.org
   Their goal is to prevent teen pregnancy by supporting values and stimulating actions that are consistent with a pregnancy-free adolescent.

National Organization of Adolescent Pregnancy, Parenting, and Prevention (NOAPP)
1319 F Street NW
Suite 401
Washington, DC 20004
(202) 783-5770
noapp@aol.com
   Promotes services designed for the prevention and resolution of problems associated with adolescent pregnancy and parenthood.

GAY, LESBIAN, BISEXUAL, TRANSGENDER, AND QUESTIONING TEENS

And no one cared that I have a full load of classes and work on writing a book and poetry slam competitions and I'm the president of the earth club and I'm trying to start a fucking Gay-Straight Alliance and just tell me to shut up. (Trope 2003, 230)

In a world where the majority of people are straight, it is essential to learn about GLBTQ issues so that you can better serve the people in your community. You can gain a general knowledge about what it means to be gay, lesbian, bisexual, or transgender by talking with community members, perhaps at a gay and lesbian center. Reading literature, nonfiction books, and news stories about GLBTQ issues will also help keep you informed. Many older GLBTQ teens rely on the library for information, and a well-informed, open-minded staff will result in a better library collection and better service. Consider the following comments when determining your own knowledge about these issues and deciding if the library is prepared to serve older GLBTQ teens:

'I've always known I was bisexual.' The speaker was a sixteen-year-old student at Cambridge Rindge and Latin High School. The occasion was the school's annual Coming-Out Day, and the announcement by Khadjihah Britton was made to an audience of 250 classmates. (Garber 1995, 16)

I worked part-time at the library, where the (doubtlessly) lesbian librarian took me aside and gave me Rubyfruit Jungle to read 'to see if it would be appropriate for the Young Adult Section' and went out of her way to get a hold of a pamphlet about 'Being Gay in High School' put together by some radical high school students in Ann Arbor. (Hutchins 1991, 135)

Generally disinterested with most aspects of high school, I focused most of my social activity on a small circle of friends, a part-time job, and the school library. I explored the shelves and found no information on bisexuality in print. (Hutchins 1991, 53)

Some GLBT teens decide to leave high school early and attend college as soon as possible. Kerry, sixteen, tells her story:

I'm going off to college a year early, and I'll be living in New York City; things should be easier than they were in high school. I might have liked to graduate with my class, but I don't think I would have made it. I probably would have dropped out if I'd had to face another year of high school. (Mastoon 1997, 30)

A 2003 National School Climate Survey found that 84% of GLBTQ students were verbally harrassed because of their sexual orientation. The survey, reported by the Gay, Lesbian, and Straight Education Network (GLSEN) at http://www.glsen.org, also found that 82.9% of faculty never or rarely intervene when witnessing the harrassment. Although many efforts have been made to improve relations between gay and straight students, there is still violence in schools and name calling.

Dominated by a teen culture of marked intolerance for difference and strong homophobia, school is a place where "fag" and "queer"

are everyday insults, where many older teens are vocal in their will-
ingness to use violence against anyone suspected of being gay. Hos-
tility is even found among some teachers and school executives
themselves. (Stover 1992, 35)

In the United States, there are some high schools specifically for gay,
lesbian, bisexual, and transgender students. The Harvey Milk School in
New York City's Greenwich Village is fully accredited and was founded
by the Hetrick-Martin Institute for Lesbian and Gay Youth. Students at
the school are able to be themselves without fear of violence or ridicule
from their peers. In Dallas, Texas, the Walt Whitman Community School
is a private school for gay students. Two educators, concerned about statistics relating to homosexual youth and destructive behavior, formed the
school after observing students harassing each other in another Dallas
school.

Resources about GLBTQ Teens

Atkins, Dawn, ed. 2002. **Bisexual Women in the Twenty-first Century**. New York:
    Harrington Park Press. This compilation of essays about women and bi-
    sexuality includes information about history, relationships, art, and psy-
    chology. One of the articles, "Bisexual Female Adolescents: A Critical
    Analysis of Past Research, and Results from a National Survey," by Stephen
    T. Russell and Hinda Seif, imparts statistical information relating to teen
    girls who are bisexual.
Cameron, Loren. 1996. **Body Alchemy: Transsexual Portraits**. San Francisco, CA:
    Cleis Press. Documents a female-to-male transsexual through photographs
    and interviews. This resource may be useful to librarians who need to learn
    more about transsexualism.
Cart, Michael. 2004. **Gay and Lesbian Fiction for Young Adults**. *Scarecrow Stud-
    ies in Young Adult Literature* no. 17. Lanham, MD: Scarecrow Press. Exam-
    ines issues faced by gay teens and provides an extensive list of resources
    for them.
Daniel, Patricia L., and Vicki J. McEntire. 1999. "Rights of Passage: Preparing Gay
    and Lesbian Youth for Their Journey into Adulthood." In **Using Literature
    to Help Troubled Teenagers Cope with Family Issues**, Joan F. Kaywell,
    ed., 193–224. Westport, CT: Greenwood Press. This chapter includes an an-
    notated bibliography of fiction and nonfiction for parents, teachers, direc-
    tors, and organizations, and curricular materials about sexual identity
    issues.

Jennings, Kevin, with Pat Shapiro. 2003. **Always My Child: A Parent's Guide to Understanding Your Gay, Lesbian, Bisexual, Transgendered, or Questioning Son or Daughter**. New York: Simon and Schuster. Focuses on the daily experiences of teens who are confused about their sexual identities and gives advice to parents for supporting their sons and daughters.

Latham, Bob. 2000. **The Invisible Minority: GLBTQ Youth at Risk**. Point Richmond, CA: Point Richmond Press. Provides a glossary about GLBTQ issues, a list of what everyone should know about homosexuality, a list of famous gays and lesbians, advice for teachers on helping GLBTQ teens, statistics, resources for further information, reports about the Kinsey Scale and sexual orientation, and court rulings related to GLBTQ youth. Provides practical advice to parents who are trying to understand their child's sexual orientation.

Linville, Darla. 2004. "Beyond Picket Fences: What Gay/Queer/LBGTQ Teens Want from the Library." **Voices of Youth Advocates** 32, no. 3 (August): 183–186. Explores ways in which librarians who serve teens can offer relevant materials and make information about sexual identity issues available in libraries.

Sanchez, Alex. 2004. "Crossing Two Bridges: Coming Out, the Power of Images in YA Lit: Remarks Adapted from Panel Discussion at the 2003 NCTE Convention." **The ALAN Review** 32, no. 1 (Fall): 56–60. Sanchez discusses his books for teens and his own experiences as a gay teen. The article includes several e-mail letters that he has received from teens and teachers.

Savin-Williams, Ritch C. 2005. **The New Gay Teenager** (*Adolescent Lives*). Cambridge, MA: Harvard University Press. The author, a professor at Cornell University, explains how modern gay teens are reluctant to label themselves and argues that the stereotype of gay teens being depressed and suicidal is false. The book explores psychological models used to study gay adolescents.

CONCLUSION

In the Newbery medal–winning novel *The Giver* by Lois Lowry, a utopian society exists, ensuring that all people are treated equally, and poverty, unemployment, and crime do not exist in this land. In this type of environment, there would be no such thing as an "extreme teen" because this segment of the population would be served so well by the public library that they would not stand out as a group needing special assistance. Since we do not live in a utopia, and since there are always bound to be different types of people needing diverse services based on individual needs, it is important for librarians to create an atmosphere of acceptance in libraries. Librarians who take the time to understand extreme teens will have a better understanding of the world around them, outside of the walls of their libraries.

WORKS CITED

Associated Press. 2000. "Students Charged in Internet Blackmail Scheme" (May 26): 1, www.ap.org.

Barson, Michael, and Steven Heller. 1998. **Teenage Confidential: An Illustrated History of the American Teen**. San Francisco: Chronicle Books.

Bowman, Cynthia Ann, and Jennifer Fike. 1999. "Adam and Eve and Pinch Me: Issues of Adolescents in Foster Care." In **Using Literature to Help Troubled Teenagers Cope with Family Issues**, Joan F. Kaywell, ed., 144. Westport, CT: Greenword Press.

Brown, Fleda. 2002. **Breathing In, Breathing Out**. Tallahassee, FL: Anhinga Press.

Burgess, Melvin. 1998. **Smack**. New York: Henry Holt.

Came, Barry. 1993. "Young, Gay—And Alone." *Maclean's* 106, no. 8 (February 22): 34.

Carter, Alden. 2004. "The Swede." In **First Crossing: Stories about Teen Immigrants**, Donald R. Gallo, ed., 142. New York: Candlewick Press.

Chapman, Kathleen. 2002. "Older Teen Runaways a Problem for DCF." *Palm Beach Post* (October 7): 1B.

Clayton, Mark. 1999. "After-school Activity? Try College." *Christian Science Monitor* 91, issue 46 (February 2): 15.

Davis, Deborah, ed. 2004. **You Look Too Young to Be a Mom: Teen Mothers Speak Out on Love, Learning, and Success**. New York: Penguin.

DeWitt, Karen. 1994. "Teen Moms Who Beat the Odds." *Essence* (August 1): 53.

Dorais, Michel. 2002. **Don't Tell: The Sexual Abuse of Boys**. Montreal: McGill-Queen's University Press.

Dorfman, Lori, and Vincent Schiraldi. 2001. "Judging from the News, You'd Think They Were a Plague." *The Los Angeles Times* (April 15): M2.

Dutton, Judy. 2002. "Why She Slept with Her Student." *Redbook* 199, issue 2 (August): 132.

Fisher, Amy, and Robbie Woliver. 2004. **If I Knew Then . . .** New York: iUniverse.

Foreman, Judy. 1999. "For Teenager, 'Confidential' is Conditional." *Boston Globe* (January 18): D1.

Gallo, Donald R., ed. 2004. **First Crossing: Stories about Teen Immigrants**. New York: Candlewick Press.

Goldberg, Elliot. 1986. "Let's Meet for Marketing." *Gloucester County Times* (May 19): A-3.

Grant, Cynthia D. 1995. **Mary Wolf**. New York: Atheneum.

———. 1998. **The White Horse**. New York: Simon and Schuster.

Guiden, Mary. 2000. "Not Your Average Teen Mom." *State Legislaturess* (February 2000): 26.

Haddix, Margaret Peterson. 1997. **Don't You Dare Read This, Mrs. Dunphrey**. New York: Aladdin Paperbacks.

Harrington-Leuker, Donna. 2002. "Teens Need Literacy Lessons, Too." *USA Today* (March 5): A3.

Head, Ann. 1967. **Mr. and Mrs. Bo Jo Jones**. New York: Putnam.

Hine, Thomas. 1999. **The Rise and Fall of the American Teenager**. New York: Avon.

Hinton, S. E. 1967. **The Outsiders**. New York: Dell.

Hull, John D. 1994. "Running Scared." *Time* 144, no. 21 (November 21): 92.

Jensen, Derrick. 2004. **Walking on Water: Reading, Writing, and Revolution**. White River Junction, VT: Chelsea Green.

Jones, Patrick. 2002. **New Directions for Library Services to Young Adults**. Appendix I. Chicago, IL: American Library Association.

Jonsson, Patrik. 2001. "Higher Standards—and More Dropouts?" *Christian Science Monitor* 93, issue 119 (May 20): 3.

Kinder, Anneka L. 2002. Survey of the States' Limited English Proficient Students and Available Educational Programs and Services 2000–2001 Summary Report. Department of Education. National Clearinghouse for English Language Acquisition and Language Instruction Educational Programs. The George Washington University. http://www.ncela.gwu.edu.

Krashen, Stephen. 2001. "Do Teenagers Like to Read? Yes!" **Reading Today** 18, no. 5 (April/May): 16.

Larry, Zakiya. 2000. "Teen Brides and Grooms Willing to Face Challenges." *Teen Appeal* (October 31), University of Memphis Department of Journalism.

Lee, Linda. 2000. **Success Without College: Why Your Child May Not Have to Go to College Right Now—and May Not Have to Go at All**. New York: Broadway Books.

Levine, Judith. 2002. **Harmful to Minors: The Perils of Protecting Children from Sex**. Minneapolis: University of Minnesota Press.

Llewellyn, Grace. 1991. **The Teenage Liberation Handbook: How to Quit School and Get a Real Life and Education**. Eugene, OR: Lowry House Publishers.

Marks, Alexandra. 2001. "US Shelters Swell—with Families; Recession and Sept. 11 are Causing More Homelessness, Which May Echo '80s Crisis." *Christian Science Monitor* 94, issue 5 (November 29): 1.

Mastoon, Alex. 2001. **The Shared Heart: Portraits and Stories Celebrating Lesbian, Gay, and Bisexual Young People**. New York: HarperTempest, 1997.

"Nation in Brief." 2000. *Washington Post* (November 9): A26.

National Endowment for the Arts. "Reading at Risk: A Survey of Literary Reading in America." Research Division Report no. 46. Washington, DC. Produced by Tom Bradshaw and Bonnie Nichols.

Nussbaum, Emily. 2000. "His Only Address Was an E-mail Account." *NY Times Magazine* (September 17): 80.

Orr, Tamra. 2003. **Violence in Our Schools: Halls of Hope, Halls of Fear**. New York: Franklin Watts.

Parker, Julie. 1995. **Everything You Need to Know about Living in a Shelter**. New York: Rosen.

Peterson, Karen S. 2002. "Sex Between Adults and Children: Child's Age and Maturity Make for Gray Areas." *USA Today* (April 17): D01.

Pierre, Robert E. 2002. "The Nation; Homeless Youths' Plight Is Perilous, Even in the Midwest; Society: Study of Runaways in Eight Heartland Cities Shows That Most Ran Away to Escape Abuse, Only to Be Assaulted on the Streets." *Los Angeles Times* (October 1): A19.

Plum-Ucci, Carol. 2002. **What Happened to Lani Garver**. New York: Harcourt.

Rebman, Renee C. 2001. **Runaway Teens: A Hot Issue**. New York: Enslow.

Rodowsky, Colby F. 1992. **Lucy Peale**. New York: Farrar, Straus and Giroux.

Salzman, Mark. 2003. **True Notebooks**. New York: Knopf.

Schaumburg, Ron. 2000. "When Homeless Teens Rode the Rails." *New York Times Upfront* 132, no. 11 (January 31): 18.

Shapiro, Joseph P. 1995. "Sins of the Fathers: It Is Adult Males Who Are Fathering the Babies Born to Teenagers." *U.S. News and World Report* (August 14): 51–52.

Soto, Gary. 1996. **Jesse**. New York: Scholastic.

Statistical Abstracts of the United States. 2003. Economics and Statistics Administration. Department of Commerce.

Stover, D. 1992. "The At-Risk Students Schools Continue to Ignore." *Education Digest* 57, issue 9 (May): 36.

Swerdlow, Joel L. 2001. "Changing America." *National Geographic* 200, issue 3 (September): 42.

Teicher, Stacy A. 1999. "When Minors Refuse Medical Treatment." *Christian Science Monitor* (February 9): 3.

Trope, Zoe. 2003. **Please, Don't Kill the Freshman: A Memoir**. New York: HarperTempest.

Vacca, Richard T. 1997. "The Benign Neglect of Adolescent Literacy." *Reading Today* 14, issue 4 (February/March): 3.

Vissing, Yvonne M. 1999. **Homeless Children: Addressing the Challenge in Rural Areas**. Education Department, Educational Research and Improvement Office, SuDoc Number: ED 1.331/2:EDO-RC-98-1 (January).

Weill, Sabrina Solin. 2002. *We're Not Monsters: Teens Speak Out about Teens in Trouble*. New York: HarperTempest.

White, Josh. 2001. "Police Say Girl Sent AOL Threats to Self; Teen Allegedly Tried to Blame Others." *Washington Post* (February 6): B.07.

Wildmon, Tim. 1998. "Boys Have Role, Too, in Curbing Teen Pregnancy." *USA Today* (January 6): 13A.

FOR FURTHER READING

"Age of the Sniper Doesn't Matter." 2002. *USA Today* (November 5).

Allison, Anthony. 1999. **Hear These Voices: Youth at the Edge of the Millennium**. New York: Dutton Children's Books.

Brozo, William G. 2002. **To Be a Boy, To Be a Reader: Engaging Teen and Preteen Boys in Active Literacy**. Newark, DE: International Reading Association.

Edwards, Bob. 2000. "Profile: Eight San Diego Teen-agers Accused of Attacking Several Elderly Mexican Migrant Workers May be Tried as Adults Under a New California Law." Morning Edition, National Public Radio (September 12).

Ferdinand, Pamela. 2002. "Seventeen an Awkward Age, N.H. Juvenile Justice Finds; In Reversal, State Moves to Raise Criminal Adulthood to Eighteen." *Washington Post* (March 27): A3.

Fredericks, Nancy. 2005. "A Day in the Life . . ." *Young Adult Library Services* 3, no. 2 (Winter): 13–14.

Gay, Ivey. 2002. "Meeting, Not Ignoring, Teen Literacy Needs." *Education Digest* 68, issue 2 (October): 23.

Greenberg, Keith Elliot. 1995. **Runaways**. Minneapolis: Lerner Publishing Group.

Grier, Terry B. 2000. "One District's Successful Efforts to Prevent Dropouts." *American School Board Journal* (May): 55–57.

Grisso, Thomas, and Robert G. Schwartz. 2000. **Youth on Trial: A Developmental Perspective on Juvenile Justice**. Chicago, IL: University of Chicago Press.

Guth, Nancy. 2001. "Adolescent Literacy: Seven Principles." **Reading Today** 18, no. 7 (August/September): 23.

Haffner, Debra W. 2001. **Beyond the Big Talk: Every Parent's Guide to Raising Sexually Healthy Teens—from Middle School to High School and Beyond**. New York: Newmarket Press.

Hall, Ellen, and Richard Handley. 2004. **High Schools in Crisis: What Every Parent Should Know**. Westport, CT: Praeger Publishers.

Hancock, Lynnell. 2000. "Framing Children in the News: The Face and Color of Youth Crime in America." In **The Public Assault on America's Children: Poverty, Violence, and Juvenile Injustice**, Valerie Polakow, ed. New York: Teachers College Press.

Jonsson, Patrik. 2001. "A New Vandal Hits US Streets: The Bored, Rich Teen." *Christian Science Monitor* 93, issue 240 (November 6): 1.

Mauro, Tony. 2002. "Should Juvenile Sniper Be Sentenced to Death?" *USA Today* (October 31): A15.

Owens, Robert E., Jr. 1998. **Queer Kids: The Challenges and Promise for Lesbian, Gay, and Bisexual Youth**. New York: Harrington Park Press.

Polakow, Valerie, ed. 2000. **The Public Assault on America's Children: Poverty, Violence, and Juvenile Injustice**. New York: Teachers College Press.

Reid, Suzanne Elizabeth. 2002. **Book Bridges for ESL Students: Using Young Adult and Children's Literature to Teach ESL**. Lanham, MD: Scarecrow Press.

Rycik, James A., and Judith L. Irvin. 2001. **What Adolescents Deserve: A Commitment to Students' Literacy Learning**. Newark, DE: International Reading Association.

Schmich, Mary, and Eric Zorn. 2002. "Is Sex with Teens Different If Adult Is a Woman?" *Chicago Tribune* (October 31): 1.

Smith, Michael W. 2002. "Reading Don't Fix No Chevys: Literacy in the Lives of Young Men." Portsmouth, NH: Heinemann.

Steinberg, Laurence. 2002. "Judging a Juvenile Killer." *Washington Post* (November 10): B7.

Vinh, Tan. 2001. "Giving School Dropouts Another Chance." *Seattle Times* (March 26).

2

OUTSIDE THE MAINSTREAM: SERVICE TO EXTREME TEENS

Beware of extreme teens in your library. You will know them when you see them. Many are tattooed and have an unnatural hair color. Likely you will see plenty of purple. Outrageous oranges. Bold blues. Some will be pushing baby strollers and holding the hands of toddlers. Some are homeless. Or homeschooled. Others are living without parents or they have decided to drop out of high school. Extreme teens will likely cause problems for your staff. Rudeness comes naturally to them. Hide the scissors.

Now, cringe. Reverse psychology was covered in Psychology 101 for a reason. Extreme teens come in all shapes and sizes, with all types of hair colors, and with different sets of circumstances pertaining to their lives. Just because teenagers are extreme does not mean that they look weird or are dangerous. Likewise, extreme teens should not instantly be seen as a threat to your library and staff. The first step to creating a positive environment is to ensure that your staff is well trained to work with all teens, regardless of their circumstances. Once the staff has a basic understanding of teens' needs, it will be easier to focus on specific services, such as library tours, bibliographic instruction, and programming.

Not only do adults often have assumptions about teens in general, they often assume that teens who do not necessarily fit the mold are problematic. Librarians may be under the impression that extreme teens do not need to use the library when, in fact, the library can be a stepping stone for extreme teens. For example, a pregnant teen may become an avid library user and thus have an easier time raising her child. High school dropouts may desperately need GED study guides and GLBTQ teens may find relevant facts, figures, and stories in literature and on Web sites. Since there is a high suicide rate among GLBTQ teens, it is imperative that librarians provide resources for this population, regardless of an individual's feelings about the subject.

Librarians may also feel that extreme teens have nothing in return to offer the library. This is far from the truth, for extreme teens can serve a role in helping you to understand different sectors of a diverse community. Extreme teens can become assets and advocates for the library. When promoting specialized library services to your library governing authority, such as the library board or a city council, consider asking an extreme teen who benefited from these services to give a brief presentation. In order to remind the library administration that extreme teens are being served, urge these teens to fill out comment cards or contact library management with positive feedback.

In addition to letting governing authorities know about specialized services, extreme teens can also become a part of the library's programming because of their unique experiences and knowledge. For example, Spanish-speaking teens might be able to assist catalogers with Spanish materials, or be part of a bilingual storytelling program for children. A homeless teen might build job and social skills, as well as self-esteem, by volunteering at the library. Pregnant and parenting teens might be able to give feedback about collection development needs or they might want to start a group at the library for teen parents who want to share child care duties.

Whether to offer special programming that is specifically directed toward extreme teens may or may not be successful. It is necessary to customize services to the needs of extreme teens, but keep in mind that it may not always be beneficial to completely segregate library services. In one sense, you may make extreme teens feel more comfortable if there are programs specifically for them, such as career planning for teen moms or computer classes for teens with low literacy skills. On the other hand, some teens might feel singled out and would rather participate in activities that are arranged for a general teen audience.

Another concern in a mixed group involves the possibility that teens who are not extreme may feel uncomfortable around those who are extreme. For example, at the Allen County Public Library in Fort Wayne, Indiana, the staff conducted a program called "Bannerama" in which teens assisted with the design of large banners. The banners, brightly colored and representing topics such as sports, music, education, and the arts, were created to hang on the walls of the Young Adults' Services Department in order to improve aesthetics and help with noise problems. The program was open to all teens, including members of the library's Teen Advisory Group. Incarcerated teens from a detention center located across the street from the library were also invited to participate. Many of these teens were not allowed to use scissors or glue because of problems with violence and substance abuse. It quickly became evident to the other teens involved that the group from the detention center was different. Some of the teens expressed their concern about working alongside the group from across the street.

The staff was quickly alerted to the problem and spoke with the teens about the importance of getting along with the others, despite their different social situations. They stressed that the teens from the detention center were being supervised by detention center staff at all times and that only the well-behaved incarcerated teens had been selected to attend the program. One of their goals was to help these teens display some tolerance and acceptance of others.

Before jumping into specific services for extreme teens, it is necessary to assess current services and programs to see how these teens are already being served. For instance, if school staff members are already conducting book discussions specifically for pregnant teens, it might not make sense for the public library to offer the same program. Instead, you can work collaboratively with the school and offer tours, booklists, and booktalks. Try to determine which needs are not being met, perhaps by conducting a survey or asking extreme teens at the library or those who are involved with some other type of group, such as a homeless shelter. Especially with this segment of teens, it may be necessary to go beyond the walls of your library building to reach them.

You may also want to duplicate benchmark programs and services that libraries have hosted in recent years. Programs for traditional teens can be adapted for extreme teens. Although extreme teens may have different needs, some will be the same, such as information about adolescent stages, growing into adulthood, possible career choices, and seeking independence. Some libraries, however, offer programs specifically geared to teens considered nontraditional by most of society.

By determining what has been successful in other libraries throughout the United States, you can brainstorm about how those programs may work in your library. A search of library literature will result in some information about programming for nontraditional teens. The four editions of *Excellence in Library Services to Young Adults: The Nation's Top Programs*, published by the American Library Association, provide practical, replicable programs that have been deemed successful and noteworthy. The programs included in the books focus on some that are pertinent to extreme teens, such as services for teen parents, outreach to incarcerated youth, book discussion groups for homeschooled teens, and programs involving the use of recorded books for teens learning English as a Second Language (Chelton 1994, 1997, 2000; McGrath 2004).

STAFF SELECTION

All library staff members, not just those whose specific job duties involve teens, need to be teen friendly because all staff and teens affect each other. For instance, if a staff member in technical services decides to intentionally place a book about teen sexuality in the adult collection, a teenager may suffer. Custodians who give teens glaring looks may have an impact on whether teens return to use the library. Reference librarians should treat teenagers like any other member of the public, and circulation staff should respect the privacy rights of minors. You need to be an advocate for extreme teens by helping staff overcome misconceptions about nontraditional teens.

Make it a practice to include a question about serving teens in every interview session for every job to garner attitudes about serving teens. If you are in a position to hire library staff, or have input in the hiring process, be sure to suggest the need to hire professionals who are sensitive to the needs of extreme teens. For instance, if your library already has an outreach program for incarcerated youth, ask job candidates if they are comfortable visiting prisons and working with teens in jail. Scenario questions can be used to determine how staff would react to specific situations. Be clear with candidates that you do not expect them to know all of the library's policies and procedures, but you are interested in how they would react in the following instances:

- While serving at the reference desk, you observe a teenager at the circulation desk, checking out several books about teen pregnancy. As the teenager walks away from the circulation desk, you hear one circulation clerk say loudly to another staff member, "Oh, kids these days! What is this world coming to?" How would you react to this situation?

- A library patron complains to you that a book about homosexuality for teenagers is inappropriate for the library's collection. How do you respond? Would you respond differently if the person complaining about the book were a staff member preparing to catalog the book for the library's collection?

- Teenagers who appear to be homeless often hang out at the library. When they ask to get library cards, circulation desk staff tell them that they need a form of identification showing a current address, and that if they are a minor, a parent must sign the application. What suggestions would you have to the library administration regarding this policy?

STAFF TRAINING

Does the library custodian interact with teens? How about the security officers, if you have them, in your library? Reference librarians, custodians, security officers, children's librarians, the library director, and all other staff members should be trained to work with teens. All staff who have some type of contact with teens should be familiar with the basic developmental stages of adolescence.

There are three stages of development—early, middle, and late—in which teens experience cognitive, psychological, physiological, and emotional changes. If teens visit libraries and are helped by staff members who are familiar with the typical teen behavioral stages, it is likely that the experience will be more positive for both the teens and the staff. In addition to training staff in the basics of adolescent development, consider ensuring that staff members know how to positively interact with those teens facing exceptional circumstances.

In-house Training

Since 1994, YALSA has administered a Serving the Underserved (SUS) training program that provides libraries with instructors for improving teen services. Training can be tailored to the specific needs of your library. Consider hiring an SUS trainer to provide your staff with information about adolescent development, outreach, collection development, programming, and reference services. SUS trainers are scattered throughout the United States. For a list of available trainers and their contact information, visit http://www.ala.org/yalsa.

The American Library Association's Office for Diversity also offers training that may be beneficial if your goal is to teach your staff to be more open-minded about diverse populations. Several of their workshops focus on specific topics such as training library services for multicultural and multilingual users, reaching out to English as a Second Language speakers, interactive diversity workshops for managers, and serving diverse youth. More information about this training is available on their Web site, http://www.ala.org/diversity.

Also, members from the Association of Specialized and Cooperative Library Agencies (ASCLA), and the Reference and User Services Association (RUSA), two divisions of the American Library Association (ALA), and ALA members affiliated with the Office for Literacy and Outreach Services (OLOS), are available to assist librarians who have questions about serving people with disabilities, literacy programs, outreach services, and serving those who are incarcerated. In order to search a directory that includes topics and librarians who can provide assistance, access the following Web site: http://cs.ala.org/ra/speakers/.

Another type of in-house training involves supplying staff with the materials and the time necessary to become familiar with professional resources. By subscribing to pertinent library science, humanities, and social science journals, or ensuring that the information is available to them online, you will provide your staff with rich resources as they serve diverse teen populations. Instead of merely subscribing to publications such as *School Library Journal*, *Voice of Youth Advocates*, *Booklist*, and *Young Adult Library Services*, share with your colleagues specific articles that relate to serving extreme teens. Consider hiring psychologists, adolescent specialists, juvenile detention center staff, and health care workers who assist pregnant and parenting teens to speak at staff meetings and training sessions. By including experts from other professions, library staff members will expand their thinking about the needs of teenagers.

Library Organizations

There are many subgroups of library associations that serve nontraditional populations, including:

- The Outreach to Teens with Special Needs Committee of YALSA, a division of ALA, addresses the needs of teens who do not or cannot use the library because of educational, legal, socioeconomic, or physical factors. http://www.ala.org/yalsa

- The Association of Special and Cooperative Library Agencies (ASCLA), a division of ALA, has a Librarians Serving Special Populations (LSSPS) section that includes a Library Services to Prisoners Forum, the purpose of which is to raise the consciousness level of people within the library and correctional communities regarding the particular library needs of all prisoners. http://www.ala.org/LSSPSTemplate.cfm?Section=LSSPS

- The Subcommittee on Library Services to the Poor and Homeless (http://www.ala.org/olos) as well as the Task Force on Hunger, Homelessness and Poverty (http://www.hhptf.org), of ALA, seeks to raise awareness regarding library services to these specialized populations.

- The Gay, Lesbian, Bisexual, and Transgendered (GLBT) Round Table of ALA supports library workers and raises awareness of issues surrounding sexual identity. http://www.ala.org/ala/glbtrt/welcomeglbtround.htm

- The Center for the Study of Rural Librarianship, founded by Clarion University of Pennsylvania, focuses on library services to those living in rural communities. http://www.clarion.edu/libsci

- The Urban Library Council is responsible for studying and expanding library services to those in urban areas. http://www.urbanlibraries.org

- The Serving Young Adults in Urban Populations Discussion Group of YALSA, a division of ALA, is for librarians who serve teens in urban areas. Also, YAL-OUT is a YALSA list for sharing information about teens outside of library walls, including homeless and incarcerated teens. To subscribe to either list, visit http://www.ala.org/yalsa.

Conferences

Programs relating to serving nontraditional teens have been conducted at national library conferences in recent years. In 2001, YALSA's president's program at the ALA annual conference was "Key to the Captive Teen," featuring author Walter Dean Myers as the speaker and a panel of librarians who serve incarcerated teenagers. The Outreach to Teens with

Special Needs Committee has conducted several beneficial programs in the past few years at conferences. In 2003 they presented "Living in the Salad Bowl: Serving Immigrant Teens" and "Taking It to the Streets: Outreach to Homeless Teens" in 2001. A panel discussion titled "Earphone English" in 2001, presented by YALSA, focused on ESL students and audiobooks. In 2000, YALSA and the GLBT Round Table held a joint preconference that focused on library services to gay youth titled "Gay Teens in the 21st Century: Access for the Future." At the 2004 ALA annual conference in Orlando, Florida, the GLBT Round Table offered a program titled "Hidden in the Stacks," that focused on library materials featuring GLBTQ themes for children and teenagers. Also in 2004, the LSSPS of ASCLA presented "Has Your Public Librarian Been to Prison?" at the ALA annual conference, which focused on library services for those who are incarcerated.

State and regional library associations also provide staff training that relates to extreme teenagers. The young adult section of the New Jersey Library Association hosted "GLBTQ Teens and Your Library: The Real Deal" at the New Jersey statewide 2004 conference. "Out of the Closet and Onto the Shelves" was presented at the Children and Young People's Division Conference of the Indiana Library Federation in 1999. Also in Indiana in 2004, "Sexual Minority Youth in the Heartland" was a workshop for librarians and educators presented at Indiana University. This small sampling of activities throughout the United States shows that librarians are concerned with the needs of extreme teens, regardless of their individual circumstances. A well-trained staff includes those who are given both the time and the funding to attend local, state, and national library conferences so that they can be better prepared to serve diverse communities.

NETWORKING

There are many opportunities for librarians to network with community groups serving extreme teens. In most communities, you can find juvenile detention centers, teens living in foster care or group homes, and advocacy groups relating to various topics. Familiarize yourself with local, state, and national organizations and agencies that serve extreme teens. For example, to better serve homeschoolers, contact the Department of Education in your state and any homeschool organizations. Not only can you promote these organizations to families, they can promote the public library to parents and teens already involved in the organizations. Publicize the library in any brochures, newsletters, or Web sites that organizations may maintain for parents and students.

Make connections with the colleges and universities offering courses to high school students. There may be opportunities for joint bibliographic instruction with the college or university library, and librarians or professors may provide public librarians with curriculum information. Some college libraries have already collaborated with public libraries and high schools in order to serve special students. In Detroit, Michigan, four high schools participated in a pilot program in which the staff communicated with area schools about expectations for incoming freshman. In Brooklyn, New York, librarians at Brooklyn College worked with honors students, teachers, and librarians in two New York City high schools and provided basic bibliographic instruction and access to the college library. The teachers then assigned projects requiring college-level research. When high school teachers, college professors, and librarians build bridges through collaborative efforts, dual-enrollment students will more likely benefit from library services.

If your personal schedule permits, consider volunteering at an agency that serves extreme teens. There may be a group of health care workers who provide specialized services to teen parents and their children. They would probably welcome assistance from a librarian. If volunteering is not an option, there may be a place for you on the board or advisory committee of a local group. For example, as a member of the More Adult Readers in Kent County (MARK) Board, I am pleased that all tutors require their students to obtain public library cards. If you do not have the time to serve in any of these capacities, try to work with agencies in your area on some level. Make them feel welcome in your library. Offer library tours to tutors and students, and consider expanding your library collection to include more materials appropriate for extreme teens.

LEARNING ABOUT ADOLESCENT STAGES

Before attempting to promote the library to any teenager, learn all you can about them. Teens go through three different stages involving cognitive, physical, social, and biological growth:

- Early: From about age eleven through age fourteen, teens go through puberty and they are moody! Their bodies are rapidly changing. Suddenly, parents are freaks. Friends are important.

Bedroom doors are slammed shut as teens demand privacy from their parents and siblings. In school, cliques do not merge. Young teens become better at arguing. Watch out, debate team!

- Middle: Those in the middle adolescence stage are typically ages fifteen and sixteen. During this time, academics and athletics typically take precedence in the lives of teens. They rush around doing homework, going to athletic practice, engaging in hobbies, and working at part-time jobs. They are beginning to drive, so they have more freedom from their parents. This also leads to the possibility of increased sexual activity, as many teens have wheels to take someone out on a date, or to the closest "No Tell" Motel. Some may have vans equipped with beds. Teens' bodies continue to develop and grow stronger during these years. They are quick thinkers and enjoy analyzing difficult and complex subjects. Watch out, poker players!

- Late: During late adolescence, when teens are approximately age seventeen through nineteen, they are preparing for adulthood. Like adults, they may be involved in a steady sexual relationship, they may be able to vote and fight for their country, or they may be married. Physically, they are almost fully grown. They have many of the same informational needs as adults. In the library they may seek books and resources on independent living, colleges, jobs, and careers. Watch out, librarians! There go all of the books on college scholarships!

During these three stages, the needs of adolescents in the library will change as well. In early adolescence, young teens are more likely to use the library as a place to hang out. Younger teens may also be more likely to attend library programs, especially if they were active in library programming as children. Teens in middle and late adolescence typically do not have as much leisure time. Programming for middle and older teens should be related to their immediate needs. For example, a seventeen-year-old may get a lot out of a program about what college will be like. Teens who stopped using the library as children might be more likely to return to the library once they acquire a driver's license and can decide for themselves if they want to use the library. On the other hand, however, older teens, not as controlled by their parents wishes, may be less likely to visit the library.

Extreme teens, like all teens, experience all three stages of adolescence. They may have a more difficult time as they strive to reach adulthood because of circumstances in their lives. Teens in early adolescence who are extreme, such as delinquents, may find it difficult to fit in at school. A sixteen-year-old who determines that he is gay may not be thrilled about attending the homecoming dance, and therefore his social needs will differ from other teens. In the late stage of adolescence, a high school student who is already attending college may have already left high school behind. While peers are planning for college, dual-enrollment students are already coping with college life. Extreme teens are like other teens in that they still experience various stages of adolescence, but they are also different in that their social, physical, and cognitive situations may not be the same as mainstream teens.

SPECIAL CONSIDERATIONS IN SERVING EXTREME TEENS

When exploring policy decisions that may have an impact on extreme teens, collaborate with your library's administration. Different types of patrons also need special consideration at times. For example, where I work, when Amish patrons wish to obtain library cards at the library, it is only logical to allow the staff more flexibility in taking care of their needs. Typically, patrons need a photo identification to get a library card; the Amish, who shun photography, are not able to provide such identification. Some of the same types of policy decisions are needed where extreme teens are concerned. Foster teens, for example, may need to gain permission from a foster parent to use the library if the biological parent is not available to sign for a library card. In some cases, social services agencies agree to take the responsibility of signing a library card application form so that foster teens can use the library. Homeless teens sometimes face problems when they try to obtain library cards, and thus it may be necessary to work with local homeless shelters to help them. Emancipated teens, who are legally separated from their parents, need to have some type of documentation that attests to their status.

Confidentiality and privacy issues are relevant when serving all teens, but are especially important for those who are nontraditional. Keep in mind that some states have laws protecting privacy and confidentiality. The reactions of the staff can be detrimental or rewarding, depending on how each situation is handled. When I presented a workshop for a multicounty library system on how to work with teenagers, I found it important to learn about the staff beforehand. Questionnaires and responses to specific scenarios are important ways to assess how staff members will handle unique situations. One questions is, "You are at the public service desk. A female teenager approaches you and asks you for books about abortion. How would you handle the situation?" One staff members' response was that she would not worry about the situation. She lived in a very small town, and she probably would know the girl. She said that she would call the girl's parents to let them know what happened. By educating your staff, and asking them to read and sign the Library Bill of Rights, and offering ongoing training on sensitive topics, situations like this one can be avoided.

THE PUBLIC LIBRARY IS OUR LIBRARY: SERVING HOMESCHOOLERS

Homeschooled teens often become regular public library users since they do not have access to a traditional school media center. If a public library collection is weak, parents and teens may need to gain access to materials through interlibrary loan. If you serve homeschooled students, consider providing them with regular tours, bibliographic instruction, and programs that are geared toward their specific curricular needs. These students may need information about electronic databases, appropriate Web pages about different school subjects, and e-mail services. Also, some libraries have book discussion groups tailored for homeschooled students.

HIGH SCHOOL IN THE MORNING AND COLLEGE IN THE EVENING: SERVING DUAL-ENROLLMENT STUDENTS

Students who attend high school and college simultaneously may need information about college life, time management, and materials related to their studies. They probably also need information about rules and regulations regarding dual enrollment and information about curriculum and course offerings at local colleges. They may need to find out whether other colleges are going to accept credits taken while they were still in high school.

Keep in mind, however, that there is some debate about whether high school students should be allowed to take college courses. One of the main arguments against the practice is that high school students are not socially capable of interacting with older students. Critics postulate that they will lose touch with friends of the same age, and that older students may expose younger students to new and different experiences for which they may not be ready. Arguments against the practice of teens attending college state that the mission of the college or university is to serve adults, not youth. When serving dual-enrollment students, consider ways in which you can help these teens stay connected with high school students. Perhaps you can offer programs targeting both populations. If your library has a summer reading program, or celebrates YALSA's Teen Read Week in October, invite dual-enrollment students to participate. Older teens in high school, as well as dual-enrollment students, may be interested in attending programs on how to use the library or develop time management skills.

FOR THOSE WHO DID NOT STAY IN SCHOOL: SERVING DROPOUTS

Think of all the teenagers in the world who have chosen to drop out of high school. Students who felt stifled in the classroom may thrive in a public library where they have the freedom to roam, explore, and become knowledgeable about many topics. Consider that by welcoming high school dropouts into the library, you may be their last chance to create lifelong readers and learners; and if you scare them away, they may never return.

Assess your attitudes toward high school dropouts; do not hold grudges against them. Instead, accept the fact that some people do not learn well in a classroom environment. Just as you need to be open-minded about materials selected for the library collection, you must also be tolerant about the people you serve in the library. Even though you may not agree with the lifestyle that other people have chosen, this should not keep you from assisting them in the library. If you see teens using the library during the school day, do not automatically assume that they are cutting school. They may have legitimate reasons to be in the library, and your assistance is important to them.

It may be beneficial to partner with local colleges or other places that offer GED training and testing to high school dropouts. GED teachers as well as students should be made aware of library materials that are available to them. Also, find out if there are employers in the area who are interested in hiring high school dropouts. Library staff and administrators may be able to work with these employers to promote the library's collection. Keep in mind that high school dropouts are not usually adults. In many states, students can drop out of high school at age sixteen. These older teens are still teenagers, and they are not yet developmentally mature. Although they have chosen to be part of the adult world, they are not yet fully capable of being adults.

In addition to helping high school dropouts, consider how you can help prevent students from dropping out in the first place. Find out if there are efforts in your local schools to keep students from dropping out and determine how the library can be involved. Jason Summey, an eighth grader at Erwin Middle School in Asheville, North Carolina, began a program to help his fellow classmates stay in school. He was inspired to begin the project when he learned that Erwin High School had the largest dropout rate in the county. He began a "Dropout Patrol" made up of students who were willing to support other students who were at risk of dropping out.

CAN JOHNNY READ YET?
LITERACY AND RELUCTANT READERS

Dear Johnny Nolastname:

Watch out! There are debates about whether you can or cannot read, whether you just choose to refrain from reading, and whether "reading" on the Internet and "reading" magazines are actually considered "reading" at all. You became famous back in 1986 when Rudolf Franz Flesch wrote a book called Why Johnny Can't Read: And What You Can Do About It. *Since that date, a book was published about why you still could not read years later. When series books by R. L. Stine and other popular young adult authors emerged, people argued whether it was useful for you to read such "trash" when you could be reading a "good" book such as* Huckleberry Finn *by Mark Twain or a Chris Crutcher novel. My advice is that you just keep on reading what you want to read. Do not let anyone stand in your way!*

Sincerely,
A Nonjudgmental Librarian Who Loves Mad *magazine*
P.S. Alfred E. Neuman for President!

This fictitious letter holds a kernel of truth in the ongoing debate about youth and their reading habits, especially teenagers. Some librarians and educators are quick to judge the reading materials of teens as unworthy, and to assume that many teenagers cannot read, dislike reading, or just will not read. Flesch's book explores why youth have difficulty learning how to read. The book has stood the test of time, and, years after it was published, researchers are still trying to determine why some youth do not read.

As a youth-serving librarian, you should support all types of reading. It is insulting to judge people based on what they read, so keep your opinion to yourself about supposedly "trashy" series books when readers, perhaps reluctant readers, are entertained and informed by these books. Some critics consider magazines, comic books, and graphic novels to be inappropriate reading materials. To promote reading, the American Library Association began producing and selling posters and bookmarks of noteworthy people reading their favorite books. Those who have been featured on the posters and bookmarks include various athletes, actors, heroes, writers, musicians, and others. Alfred E. Neuman, a character featured in *Mad* magazine, is one such celebrity. Staff of the American Library Association should be commended for including Alfred E. Neuman because on the poster and the bookmark he pretends to be reading *A Beginner's Guide to Spelling* when he is actually hiding—and reading—*Mad* magazine. The word "read," in a typical *Mad*-type spoof, is spelled "reed" with the second "e" crossed out in red and corrected with the appropriate "a." Featuring a magazine on the "read" posters and bookmarks sends a positive message to youth and adults: Reading magazines is okay, and yes, this is also considered reading.

In 2001, the theme of YALSA's Teen Read Week was "Get Graphic @ Your Library," which featured comic books and graphic novels. Most likely, this sent a positive message to teens, librarians, parents, and educators, that these types of materials can be enjoyed as reading materials. When you design programs and services for young adults, try to be as flexible as possible, especially as you determine what could and should be considered reading material. Many libraries have begun to reward teenagers for the amount of time that they spend reading instead of how many books they read. That way, zines, e-books, articles, information and newspapers on the Internet, and anything else that can be read is counted.

IS THIS LAND YOUR LAND?
ESL AND IMMIGRANT TEENS

People could see I was a newcomer. The first struggle was the language. I was very sad going to school and not being able to communicate. For a time, I became mute. I just listened, and I couldn't figure out even a word of what they were saying. ("Teen Immigrants: 5 American Stories," from *In the Mix*, the weekly PBS teen series. *Writing* 25, issue 1 [September 2002: 10])

If you have spoken English for your entire life in a country where English is the primary language, try to imagine what it would be like to be an ESL student. Think about all the errands you complete in a single week and how difficult it would be to accomplish these tasks in a place where you do not speak the language. When working with ESL teens, be patient and try to understand that they will probably need more assistance than other library users.

If you live in an area where there are a lot of ESL teens, there already may be good services in place for this segment of the population. It may be easy to connect with local social service agencies and schools in order to enhance existing programs. You could, for example, give public library tours to ESL teens in conjunction with school librarians and guidance counselors who may have a lot of contact with these teens. Some libraries have administered book discussion groups for ESL teens. It has been beneficial for some librarians to use recorded books with ESL teens because they help them become more familiar with the English language.

If there are few ESL teens in your area, you could consider contacting librarians in other parts of the country who serve a large population of ESL teens for ideas about programs and other services. You can replicate these programs in your own library, perhaps on a smaller scale depending on the number of participants. There has been debate throughout the library world about what is more important in library programming—quality or quantity. Oftentimes, librarians will be proud that they were able to attract a lot of people to a program. But if the event was overcrowded, though, quality should overrule quantity. This is an especially significant factor with ESL teens because they are going to need a lot of individual attention, particularly if the foreign language skills of library staff members are limited.

When promoting the library and focusing on the English language, do not forget that these teens may also crave information and materials in their native languages. By conducting research in your local area and working with other groups who serve ESL teens, you may find out more about the different languages they speak.

The following information is about ESL teens and provides samples of programs and services throughout the United States. You may be able to adapt these programs for use with teens in your area or use this information to better serve this segment of the extreme teen population:

- The Berkeley (CA) Public Library and Berkeley High School collaborated to help ESL teens improve their knowledge of the English language. They formed a group, which meets once a week and listens to recorded books in order to improve their English language skills. More information about this program is available in Francisca Goldsmith, "Earphone English" (*School Library Journal* 48, no. 5 [May 2002]: 50–53).

- Students involved in the audiobook program in Berkeley, California, were invited to attend the ALA Annual Conference in 2001, held in San Francisco. They were part of a panel discussion along with Pam Muñoz Ryan, author of *Esperanza Rising* (2000). For more information, read "How Audiobooks Helped Us to Listen, Speak, and Earn a Cool Trip" (*Voice of Youth Advocates* 24, no. 5 [December 2001]: 345). In recent years, YALSA has made youth participation a priority. Teens are asked to comment on books and videos that are then added to "best of" and "selection" lists. Many panels at conferences include teenagers who offer their insight about library services. Some teenagers also write for professional library journals and are part of the review process for nonfiction and fiction works. Think about what your library is doing for teens, how you can share your ideas on a local, state, or national level, and involve the teens who benefit from your services.

- In many families with parents who speak languages other than English, children and teens often take on the adult role and become communicators for their parents. More information about this trend is available in the article "The Young Voice of the Family; When Adults Can Speak Little English, Children Take On a Grown-Up Role" (*Washington Post*, April 12, 2000, B3). Consider the effect of this trend on public library users, and what kinds of programs could be created to help teens who act as the adult in the family because of language barriers. Services could include life-skills information to assist teens help their parents adjust to life in a new country.

- In Prince William County, Virginia, former ESL students are hired to work as ESL student assistants. An article in *Education Week* features Reyhaneh Fathieh, a college sophomore, who entered U.S. schools at age eleven and had to learn English. As a student assistant during the summer months, she is responsible for helping younger students become familiar with English and American culture. Assistants also ensure that students speak English, not Spanish, while working in small group settings. More information is available in "Former ESL Students Tapped as Class Aides" (*Education Week* 23, no. 43 [July 28, 2004]: 12). This arrangement could be useful to public librarians who seek to better serve ESL teens. Student assistants could collaborate with librarians about programs and services and could possibly work as consultants for the library. The library could then promote its services to high school students involved in ESL classes.

- Gail Junion-Metz, author of "Learning a Language Online" (*School Library Journal* 49, no. 1 [January 2003]: 30), discusses Web sites that are useful to ESL teens. Students need pictorial representations to learn languages and the Internet offers some excellent resources, including picture dictionaries, flash cards, and crossword puzzles. Librarians could offer computer training classes to ESL teens that specifically focus on the preselected Web sites mentioned in this article.

- Teens from other countries may be interested in teaching others about their culture and writing about their former lives. In the article "Changing America" (*National Geographic* 200, no. 3 [September 2001]: 42), author Joel L. Swerdlow focuses on ESL students at J.E.B. Stuart High School in Falls Church, Virginia. Swerdlow writes, "They may sense that they are losing their family stories in the blender. Students here come from places where there's war, civil unrest, or extreme poverty." Public librarians could connect with school librarians and English teachers to determine the needs of ESL students who want to use creative outlets, such as writing and art, to express their feelings about their new lives in America, while respecting and recording information about their past.

IT IS A BIG, SCARY WORLD OUT THERE:
SERVING HOMELESS AND RUNAWAY TEENS

"If it were not for the help of librarians, I would still be living on the street." A man who previously had been homeless said these words to me. We were riding in a bus from New Jersey to Philadelphia. It was 1994, and I was completing an internship at the Free Library of Philadelphia as part of my coursework to earn a graduate degree in library science. The man thanked me for deciding to become a librarian. He said that had it not been for librarians, he never would have gotten his life back together. Feeling a bit odd, since I was not yet a librarian, I smiled and told him that I appreciated his comment. Somewhere in South Jersey there are librarians who need to be thanked for helping a former homeless man.

At the 2001 American Library Association annual conference in San Francisco, California, a program titled "Taking It to the Streets: Outreach to Homeless Teens," was sponsored by the YALSA Special Needs Committee. Several panelist members helped answer the question, "What is it like to be a homeless teen today and how can librarians better serve this growing population?" Teens from the Larkin Street Youth Center in San Francisco, were part of the panel that offered advice to youth services librarians. They gave librarians the following suggestions for serving homeless teens:

- Provide library tours for homeless youth to showcase programs, services and collections.
- Create liberal in-house policies and procedures especially for homeless youth. For example, waive fines for overdue and lost books; allow food and beverages in the library; give homeless teens the option of using youth centers as their primary address when applying for a library card.
- Offer Web design classes and other programs that would interest teens.
- Provide homeless youth with a place to hang out.
- Realize that the lives of homeless youth are in a constant state of flux.

Although the suggestions from the teenagers in San Francisco are worth considering, every community is different. Consider listening to the homeless teens and runaways in your community. Find out how your library can better serve them. Whether your library is in a rural, suburban, or urban environment, it is highly likely that homeless people and runaways do exist in your community. Consider broadening the volunteer program at your library to involve teens living in shelters, or begin a volunteer program specifically for this population. Not only will you benefit from the volunteers' accomplishments, but also a broader range of people will be exposed to public library services.

Your library should be a place of acceptance of homeless people, of all ages. Work with the library administration to ensure that homeless people are not needlessly discriminated against. Become familiar with local, state, and national laws relating to homelessness and runaways. In 1977, Congress passed the Runaway Homeless Youth Act, making it illegal to arrest a child simply because he or she has run away from home. The Stewart B. McKinney Homeless Assistance Act of 1987 required all fifty states to take steps that would guarantee all homeless children the same right to a "free and appropriate public education" as children who are not homeless.

Learn about community programs that assist homeless teens and runaways. If these services do not exist in your community, work with other youth service advocates to create programs modeled after services in other places in the United States. The following are some programs for homeless and runaway teens. Think about how you could adapt these programs to fit the needs of your community.

- In Flint, Michigan, at-risk males and females ages seventeen through twenty can participate in the Transitional Living Program. The purpose of the program is to empower young adults to take control of their lives by offering them support, training, and case management. Participants must attend school or obtain a GED, maintain employment, set aside at least 60 percent of their income to establish independent living, and abide by house rules. Participants are provided with medical screenings and tutoring.

- The Toronto (Canada) Public Library worked with shelters and youth agencies in 1999 to publish *Young Voices from the Streets*, a twenty-seven-page booklet reflecting the experience of homelessness through stories and poems written by teenagers.

- Beginning in 1989, in Spokane, Washington, homeless children and their families were provided with educational services. The program was a collaborative effort between the local YWCA, homeless shelters, and Spokane Public Schools. Edith L. Sims, facilitator of the Homeless Education Program, gave congressional testimony supporting the program in September 2000.

- In Virginia, a statewide program called Project Hope helps keep homeless children in public schools. According to an article by Vaishali Honawar in the *Washington Times* (2001), the number of children in public schools rose from 13,000 in the mid-1990s to 17,000 between 1999 and 2000. Every afternoon after school in Fairfax County, Virginia, a public school bus picks up homeless children from school and drops them off at a homeless shelter. Books donated by libraries are kept at the shelter. Sometimes workers at the shelter take children on trips to the public library.

- Each Sunday at the Fairmont Hotel in San Jose, California, homeless teens are given a free lunch thanks to members of the Home Church and the Evangelical Christian Fellowship in San Jose and the Vineyard Church in San Francisco. The church groups also provide the teens with donated toiletries.

BUSTED:
SERVING DELINQUENT AND
INCARCERATED TEENS

The lights in the room dimmed and some music came over the intercom. It was classical, I knew that much, but I didn't know what kind. It was nice. Then a voice began to read, a grandmotherly sort of voice, warm and quiet. (Ferris, 1998)

Sixteen-year-old Dallas is serving a six-month sentence in a girls' rehabilitation center after robbing a convenience store. During her incarceration, volunteers read stories to her before bedtime. She ponders the fact that she has no recollection of anyone ever reading her a bedtime story. Once you have a well-trained staff, an extensive collection of library materials, and appropriate services for extreme teenagers, it is time to reach out to those who cannot visit your library, like Dallas. Unlike traditional teens, extreme teens may not be able to physically visit the library.

Helping Juvenile Delinquents

Many libraries throughout the United States have begun outreach programs to teens in juvenile detention centers. They provide a range of services, including deposit collections of library materials, readers' advisory, and programming. Collections in alternative facilities are especially important for teens who cannot visit the public library but need access to information and recreational reading materials. Some programs that would typically be conducted inside library walls, such as summer reading activities, can also be duplicated in detention centers. One example is the Ocean County Library System in Toms River, New Jersey. For the past three years, librarians employed by the library system have been providing service to teens at the Ocean County Juvenile Detention Center. According to Jeri Triano, Teen Services Librarian in Brick, New Jersey, much of her time at the detention center is spent talking about books and suggesting other titles to read. The collection consists of approximately 1,700 volumes. In addition to a budget of approximately $2,500 that is supplied by the juvenile detention center administration, discarded books from branches throughout the library system are given to the facility. Book discussions are held each month, short stories are read to the teens, online tours of the library's Web site are given, and teens can also obtain library cards.

Leaders in the field of young adult librarianship are aware of the importance of reaching out to incarcerated teens. Mary Arnold, past YALSA president, chose this topic of serving teens as her focus in 2001: "Can you reach troubled teens who can't get to the library? Find out how, from some of the leaders of award-winning programs targeted at teens in detention centers." This was the blurb for the *YALSA President's Program 2001: The Key to the Captive Teen*, held at the American Library Association's annual conference in San Francisco, California. After a speech by Walter Dean Myers, winner of the 2000 Michael L. Printz Award for *Monster*, the audience learned about programs at the various libraries. Plenty of handouts relating to juvenile delinquent outreach programs were distributed. Here are some examples of what some libraries are doing:

- Johnson County Library, Shawnee Mission, Kansas. "Read to Succeed" provides a collection of paperback books for residents in the County Juvenile Detention Center. Library staff members also facilitate theme-based literature programs, visit the center twice a month, give booktalks and book reviews, and read aloud. A short story or chapter from a book is read to a group of ten to fifteen teens.

- Hennepin County Library, Minnetonka, Minnesota. The goal of the "Great Transitions: Struggle Change Achieve" program is to engage young people in the juvenile corrections system with the library and its array of resources and services in order to help them become avid readers and competent information seekers. The program shows adjudicated youth how the library can help as they struggle, learn to change, and ultimately achieve their goals.

- N. A. Chaderjian Youth Correctional Facility, Stockton, California. The California Youth Authority operates several institutions and camps for youth offenders. The Youth Authority provides education, training, and treatment services for youthful offenders committed there by the courts. The N. A. Chaderjian Youth Correctional Facility serves males between ages eighteen and twenty-five.

- Allen County Public Library, Fort Wayne, Indiana. The Teen Agency Program (TAP) provides brand-new paperback books and several magazine titles to six different agencies, including three juvenile detention centers. The materials are kept permanently at the facilities. As part of the TAP program, librarians perform booktalks to incarcerated youth, and teens participate in the summer reading program. At Wood Youth Center, a high-security detention center, one of three serviced by Allen County Public Library, inmates read and listened to *Monster* by Walter Dean Myers, using materials purchased by the library. The following questions were asked in order to begin the discussion of the book:

1. Do you think that the book *Monster* by Walter Dean Myers is realistic? Why or why not?

2. Two characters admit to selling cigarettes to get out of jail early. How realistic is this situation? How realistic is it for friends to rat on each other?

3. Is the movie-making format confusing?

4. If you listened to the book on tape, did you enjoy listening instead of reading, and if so, why?

5. Do you think that Steve Harmon is guilty of being an accomplice to the murder?

6. Why do you think that the defense attorney refused to hug Steve Harmon at the end of his trial?

7. The book is set in Harlem. Could this story take place in Fort Wayne?

8. Walter Dean Myers also wrote an autobiography called *Bad Boy: A Memoir*. On page 131 he says, "I could open the textbooks, I could read the assignments, but then I would be drawn back to my own writing or reading." Are you surprised that Myers has been able to write many books even though he was unable to complete homework assignments while in school?

9. On page 42 of his autobiography, Myers says that "As much as I enjoyed reading, in the world in which I was living it had to be a secret vice. When I brought books home from the library, I would sometimes run into older kids who would tease me about my reading." In this passage, Myers explains why he had to hide the fact that he liked to read. Do you find that you are more likely to read while you are incarcerated compared with when you are not locked up?

10. On page 100 of his autobiography, Myers writes that "Books are often touted by librarians as vehicles to carry you far away. I most often saw them as a way of hiding one self inside the other. What I had to hide was the self who was a reader, who loved poetry." If you are a person who likes to read, would other people be surprised to know this about you? If you like to read poetry, do you feel as though you need to hide this from other people, and if so, why?

11. In an interview with *Booklist*, Myers said that when interviewing prisoners he learned that "They all knew why they were in jail; they knew what crimes they had committed or had been accused of committing; but they really never seemed to be sure of the path that had got them there." How do you feel about this statement? Do you think that Myers is accurate in his description of prisoners?

12. If you have any advice for people who want to help teenagers, please add your comments below.

13. If you have any other comments about the book, about prison, about reading, or just about life, please write them below.

Providing Outreach to Incarcerated Teens

If you are planning to begin an outreach program to teens who reside in juvenile detention centers, one of your first priorities should be to develop a collection development policy that addresses the needs of this population. The staff at the detention center should have a say in this policy. They may have regulations that determine what can be brought into the center, or they may decide that some material is inappropriate. Although magazines, comic books, and graphic novels are usually popular with juvenile delinquents, do not be surprised if the staff removes some of the material inside the magazines. Many staff members believe that gang-related material will cause problems among inmates, as well as any extremely violent material. Providing the *Sports Illustrated* swimsuit issue to teens may cause a riot in the detention center. Get to know the contact person at the juvenile detention center to make sure that you are providing material that is acceptable under the center's policies, and is the most beneficial for the teens there. Ask for feedback from the contact person and the inmates about whether the outreach program is beneficial and how it can be improved.

There is usually a wide range of reading abilities and maturity levels among teens in detention centers. While some seventeen-year-olds may have difficulty getting through a book intended for younger children, other thirteen-year-olds may have already read all of the books published by Clive Barker, James Patterson, and H. G. Wells. Familiarize yourself with books published for children, teens, and adults, and make sure your collection reflects all reading levels. Many inmates are extremely intelligent, and some are very well-read. Just because they have committed a crime does not mean that they are intellectually unreachable, ineducable, or unable to appreciate literature. Many young males love to read poetry. Other popular topics with juvenile delinquents include self-help books, the *Chicken Soup* books, sports, cars, contemporary issues, music, books about criminals who have made stupid mistakes, and current events. Some juvenile delinquents are not allowed to watch the news, so they learn about current events by reading magazines.

You will need to determine the format of the materials that you are going to supply to the incarcerated teens. Paperback books are usually supplied to detention centers instead of hardcovers, since the latter can be used as weapons. In some cases, depending on the reading abilities of the teens, you may want to invest more in recorded books instead of printed books.

When visiting a detention center, leave all personal items in your car. Obviously, you cannot leave your keys in your car, but you can leave them with detention center staff in a secure location on entering the building. Items that may seem harmless to you could become a weapon, such as a ballpoint pen. Exceptions to the rule about bringing personal items into a detention center can sometimes be made by contacting the staff in advance of a visit. When I performed a booktalk of *Forged by Fire* (1997) by Sharon Draper at Wood Youth Center in Indiana, I wanted to flick my Bic as a prop. I was granted permission provided that I kept track of the Bic lighter at all times.

Most outreach services use straightforward measures to determine what is being read and how often. A simple hash-mark system may be the simplest and most effective way of keeping track, since you probably will not have access to any type of automated circulation system in a detention center. For the sake of confidentiality, some detention centers may not supply librarians with the names of the inmates and the titles of what they are reading.

The length of stay in juvenile detention centers varies greatly. Some inmates are there for a few days, waiting to go to court, while others are there completing long-term sentences. Although you may see the same faces during multiple visits, in most instances, a new crop of teens will be in the detention center on a rotating basis. When teens are released from juvenile detention centers, they may decide to visit the library. By promoting your library through outreach programs, you may be inspiring incarcerated teens to become lifelong library users.

Many juvenile justice systems in the United States also operate as educational agencies, in that the systems are responsible for educating incarcerated youth. In some states, public education is provided until age twenty-one, but in the juvenile justice system, agencies define children and youth up to age eighteen. Some detention centers do not have libraries at all. Some reading material may be available as part of the classroom library. The collection of library materials provided by the public library may be the only resources that incarcerated youth and staff can access. Some facilities do not allow any access to the Internet, and this may be a difficulty if library personnel or educators intend to teach information literacy to juvenile delinquents.

If you are responsible for determining which staff members will visit juvenile detention centers, or if you are interviewing potential staff members who may be given the responsibility of working with delinquents, make sure that they are the right people for the job. If you are serving this population you need to be open-minded and nonjudgmental. If you have personal hang-ups about serving this population, or you or one of your close family members have been the victim of a serious crime, it may be difficult for you to serve delinquent teens.

On the other hand, if you do choose to serve this population, you may feel that you have made a great difference in the lives of incarcerated

---

Extreme Teen Tidbits: I'm a Juvie Hall Junkie!

Imagine (Parody by Sheila B. Anderson)

Imagine there are no discipline problems
It's easy if you try
No spitballs flying
Above us, only sky
Imagine all the teenagers
Reading every day . . .
Ah-ha ah ah ah
Imagine twelve students per teacher
It isn't hard to do
Nothing to kill or die for
And no empty stomachs, too
Imagine all the teenagers
Reading *A Separate Peace* . . .
Yoo-hoo ooh ooh
You may say I'm a juvie hall junkie
But I'm not the only one
I hope some day you will join us
And begin outreach to delinquent teens
Imagine no possessions
I wonder if you can
No need for greed or hunger
A brotherhood of man
Imagine all the teenagers
Sharing all the magazines
Yoo-hoo ooh ooh ooh
You may say I'm a juvie hall junkie
But I'm not the only one
I hope someday you will join us
And the world will live as one

Extreme Teen Tidbits: Responses from Teens at the Ocean County Juvenile Detention Center

- "I never used to read, now I don't mind it so much."
- "No matter what I ask for, Miss Jeri will find it, she even gave me one of her own books to read one day."
- "I used my own library card to place a hold for a book I wanted to read, then I got it the next week. Pretty good service."
- "Reading passes time, without it, I don't know what I would do in this place."
- "My mom will be so happy that I'm reading so much."

Extreme Teen Tidbits: A Glimpse Inside the Northeast Juvenile Detention Center in Fort Wayne, Indiana

1. The front of the building brandishes a message: " 'You can not solve a problem with the same kind of thinking that caused the problem!' Albert Einstein"
2. The building is 46,000 square feet and the gym is 6,000 square feet.
3. There is a counseling area for anger management, decision making, and parenting skills.
4. The activity area includes equipment for playing chess, pool, weight lifting, foosball, and table tennis.
5. A sign stating "New Books Provided by the Allen County Public Library" hangs near where the new books are located.

---

teens. You will not think about the fact that the people you are assisting may be rapists, murderers, pedophiles, or arsonists. Instead, you will remember that when you walked into the juvenile detention center, the inmates were delighted to see you. They were, literally, a "captive" audience. They were attentive for two reasons: first, they had to be, or else the guards would be on them in a matter of moments, and second, they were genuinely glad to see you, someone from the outside who cared, who was open-minded, with brand-new books and magazines to open their minds from confinement.

**Extreme Teen Tidbits: How Juvenile Center Employees
Responded When Asked, "What should librarians know about
working with delinquent teens?"**

1. "They know the difference between right and wrong, but they choose not to behave."

2. "Forget what you've seen on TV."

3. "They all need to feel positive about something."

4. "They are all very needy."

5. "There are many surprises and shocking stories about the backgrounds of the inmates."

6. "For many, being here is better because they have food and adults who care."

7. "It's not so bad here compared to living in a car."

8. "We practically raise some of these kids."

9. "Use your first names so that you're not looked up in the phone book."

10. "Security is not an issue. This is the safest school in the city."

FREE AT LAST:
SERVING EMANCIPATED TEENS

In my wallet was my Purley Public Library card. I didn't figure it would work here, but it showed I was an upstanding person at least. "My. All the way from Texas," the library lady said, pushing my card back across the counter. "Did you move here with family?" Was that a fair question? Would she ask it of a grown person? (Hobbs, 2004, 41–42)

Emancipated teens are legally separated from their parents. It is important to raise your awareness of state and local laws about emancipated teenagers and with organizations that assist them. Work with your state library agency or state library association to create guidelines for serving young adults, and speak up for emancipated teenagers, as librarians did in New Jersey. The "Guidelines for Young Adult Services in Public Libraries of New Jersey" (2002) in the section dealing with outreach, included emancipated minors as a group that should be served by librarians.

Fellow librarian John P. Bradford and I conducted research on how state library agencies and state library associations support young adult library services and found that very few states have created statewide guidelines for services to young adults. For more information about our findings, refer to the professional development section of the YALSA Web page. You may also refer to the article titled "Frances Henne/YALSA/VOYA Research Grant Results: State-Level Commitment to Public Library Services to Young Adults," that John P. Bradford and I wrote, published in the spring 2001 issue of *Journal of Youth Services in Libraries*.

When working with teenagers in the library, be mindful of the concept of emancipation. Do not stereotype all teenagers as people who are living with their parents and relying on their decisions. If a parental signature is required for those under age eighteen to obtain a library card or use the Internet, it may be necessary to work with library administrators to ensure that emancipated teenagers are not exempt from library privileges. If a teenager has become emancipated and is legally responsible for his or her actions, the public library should make special arrangements for this segment of the teen population. In some instances, emancipated teens may be caring for younger siblings, such as the situation described in *Chicago Blues* (1995) by Julie Reece Deaver. On page nine of the novel, eleven-year-old Marnie protests having to live with her sister, and one of her many reasons is, "I left my library card at home." Lissa, her seventeen-year-old sister, tells Marnie that she will get her a new library card. How difficult would this be in your library? Would the staff allow a seventeen-year-old to be responsible for the library account of an eleven-year-old sibling?

WITH THIS RING: SERVING MARRIED AND COHABITATING TEENS

We've already picked our bridal party, and we've created a registry with our dinnerware and stuff. It's weird to be registering for toasters when my friends are buying clothes and CDs. But I've always

been mature for my age. I started picking colleges when I was nine!
(Michelle Hainer, "I'm 17 and I'm Getting Married," 182)

Like other married couples or people who are engaged to be married,
teenagers need the same type of information and service from public libraries, perhaps with even more guidance. Whereas someone in their
twenties or older, who has experienced life for a little bit longer, may be
more mature and ready to settle down, teens who decide to get married
may need information about how to succeed in marriage. Like other married couples, teenage couples may be interested in checking out library
resources or attending programs on successful marriages, relationships,
budgets, nutrition, and other topics associated with independent living.
It is likely that they will also need information about wedding planning,
bridal attire and customs, and legal matters.

To better serve engaged and married teens, learn about teen marriage
laws in your state and surrounding states, and become knowledgeable
about changes in laws that may have an impact on teenagers who are
married. For example, teens as young as age fourteen have traveled from
Georgia to Heflin, Alabama, in order to be married at the House of Prayer
because the legal age for marriage in Georgia is sixteen but the legal age
in Alabama is fourteen. "Georgia law recognizes marriages performed out
of state only if they could have been legally performed in the state," says
Ted Hall, an attorney who is featured in an *Atlanta Constitution* (Judd
2001, A1) article about whether the marriages of Georgia teens who travel
to Alabama for the weddings are legal.

Maryland has also had controversy surrounding teen marriage laws. In
1999, state legislators faced a difficult dilemma when trying to pass a bill
that would prohibit anyone age fourteen or younger from getting married. "They note that the law would still allow 15-year-old girls to get
married if they are pregnant—a potential conflict, they argue, with the
state's statutory rape laws, which sets the legal age for consent to sex at
16," writes Amy Argetsinger in the *Washington Post* (1999, C4). Legislators in Maryland finally voted to allow anyone who is pregnant and between the ages of fifteen and seventeen to marry without parental
consent.

GLBTQ teens may also have concerns about marriage, especially with
respect to legal statutes in individual states. The issue of gay marriage is
written about not only in the media on a regular basis, but also is an ongoing debate in state legislatures. GLBTQ teens may dream about being

able to be married just like straight teens. As laws about gay marriage continue to unfold, librarians should begin to prepare to serve extreme teens who are gay and want to get married. Providing access to news sites and electronic databases with full-text articles will help GLBTQ remain informed about legislation.

WHEN THE CONDOM (AND THE WATER) BREAKS: SERVING PREGNANT AND PARENTING TEENS

Within our libraries, we need to formalize policies and procedures for dealing with sexuality issues and young people. Collection development and established procedures outlining what to do when a patron comes seeking help need to be part of these policies. Planning and preparation, that is taking a proactive stance, will make this easier. (Gross 1997, 36)

In this article, author Melissa Gross gives advice for providing library services to pregnant teens. As librarians, you have a great opportunity to help pregnant teens, parenting teens, and their children. Since money is typically tight for most teen parents, material provided at the public library is extremely valuable for this segment of the population, so make sure that you and other staff members make them feel welcome.

To help pregnant and parenting teens, learn about local programs that support teen parents and work with these groups to promote library services. In California, there are several teen father programs available, including "Con Los Padres," "Proud Fathers of the Hood," and "Role of Men." They are described in an article by Carla Rivera, "The State: Programs Help Train Young Fathers in Parenthood and Cultural Heritage Services; The Lessons and Mentoring Are Directed at Ethnic Groups That Often Lack Role Models in Their Own Upbringing," published in the *Los Angeles Times* (2002, B6). The programs teach young men why it is important to be involved in their children's lives, explain responsibilities such as custody and child support, and provide information about education and vocational training. In Roanoke, Virginia, "Reaching Out to Adolescent Dads" (ROAD) assists teen fathers in sustaining relationships with their children, finishing school, and gaining job skills. "MELD (Minnesota Early Learning Design) for Young Dads," based in Minneapolis, provides support for teen fathers who want to be more active in their children's lives. Teen fathers are provided with stress relief, child health and development classes, and assistance with careers.

Preproduced posters, postcards, and pamphlets are available for distribution from organizations and agencies that assist pregnant and parenting teens, and those that work to prevent teen pregnancy. The National Campaign to Prevent Teen Pregnancy at http://www.teenpregnancy.org is one example of an organization that produces posters and postcards directed at teens in an effort to curb teen pregnancy. They have also created tip sheets on topics that teens want parents to know about teen pregnancy, what teens want other teens to know about preventing pregnancy, and information for parents who want to help their children avoid teen pregnancy. Also, include local pregnancy and parenting organizations in your dissemination of information. Put these free items in a section of the library where teens will not be embarrassed to take the materials.

Provide programs specifically aimed at both teen parents and pregnant teens, mothers and fathers. If there are no special services for teen fathers in your area, try working with health care workers, social workers, and educators to begin such programs. Consider working with children's librarians in order to offer story times for children of teenagers. Invite pregnant and parenting teens to the library to give a tour of the library's facilities and promote library materials designed for this segment of the population. Morning Glory Press sells board games specifically for pregnant and parenting teens who are learning parenting skills. These could be used as part of a program for teenagers. Morning Glory Press also publishes books about teen pregnancy and book discussion guides for fictional works, such as author Marilyn Reynolds' True-to-Life series from Hamilton High books. Consider holding book discussion groups for teens who are parents or are about to become parents. If not enough staff is available for this, have the materials available for youth service workers in other fields who may wish to focus on literature about pregnant and parenting teens.

Be prepared to provide information and referral services to teens who may need to connect with local agencies and organizations that provide assistance to rape victims, abortion services, abortion alternatives, pregnancy, and parenting, even if your personal feelings conflict with these issues. Pregnant teens may need information about birth control, tutoring, job skills and job placement, prenatal care, housing referrals, and legal assistance.

Consider providing outreach services to pregnant and parenting teens who may find it difficult or embarrassing to visit the library. You will also want to contact other youth service workers, including health care workers and educators, on local, state, and national levels to determine the types of programs that are available for pregnant and parenting teens. For example, Graduation, Reality, and Dual-Role Skills (GRAD) is a program in various parts of the country, typically in high school home economics courses, that aims to keep pregnant and parenting teens in school, with the additional goals of encouraging good health care practices and helping young parents set career goals. The TeenAge Parent Program (TAPP) is a program in various parts of the United States that typically provides pregnant teens with information and resources for improving parenting skills, continuing educational and vocational goals, and preventing subsequent pregnancies. TAPP is offered to teens through schools and agencies. The School-to-Work Opportunities Act sometimes provides funding that can be used to help pregnant and parenting teens, as reported in *Books, Babies, and School-Age Parents: How to Teach Pregnant and Parenting Teens to Succeed* by Jeanne Warren Lindsay (1997).

NOT JUST FOR THE BIRDS AND THE BEES: SEXUALITY

Opponents of government regulation of the Net usually maintain that parents, not the state, should decide what their children see and read. But there are some adults who believe kids can make their own decisions. (Levine, 2002, 17)

Some library staff members encounter parents, community members, and even library colleagues who do not believe that it is the duty of the public library to provide information about sex to teenagers. It is important, however, to remember that teens crave information, and the library is in a position to ensure that the information they get about sexuality is accurate and nonjudgmental. Promiscuous teens, or, at the other end of the spectrum, teens who have taken abstinence pledges, may be considered extreme depending on your community. In some areas, a higher percentage of teens engage in sexual activity, whereas teens in other locations have decided to remain abstinent. Librarians, of course, are not in a position to obtain details about the sex lives of teens who use the library, but they can provide information pertaining to sexuality. It is vital that public libraries maintain an up-to-date, accurate collection of materials relating to all aspects of sexuality, including contraception, diseases, abstinence, abortion, and pregnancy.

OUT AND PROUD:
SERVING GAY, LESBIAN, BISEXUAL,
TRANSGENDER, AND QUESTIONING TEENS

The next time you have a family reunion, a corporate engagement, a party or are walking down the street, remember that one of every 15 people you see has the potential to be a homosexual, statistically anyway. (Reed, 2004, A5)

Shannon Reed, age seventeen, a senior at Milford High School in Milford, Delaware, wrote a guest opinion for the local newspaper in support of House Bill 99, which would ban discrimination based on sexual orientation in areas such as housing, public accommodations, and employment. The bill, which has not yet passed, will add sexual orientation protection to state laws that already safeguard people from discrimination on the basis of race, color, national origin, religion, gender, marital and family status, age, and disability. At age seventeen, Reed has a clear opinion about the rights of GLBTQ people, which may be surprising to some adults, especially those who do not have a lot of contact with teenagers. Library staff members should understand that the critical thinking skills of teenagers, especially older teenagers, are more developed than younger teens. These teens are more likely to have strong opinions about social issues and social justice. One way to learn about the community is by reading the newspaper, as this guest opinion shows. There were negative responses to Mr. Reed's article, and reading them were just as helpful in learning more about the pulse of the community.

Post hotline numbers on library bulletin boards of organizations that assist GLBTQ teens, such as information about gay community centers and youth groups, along with emergency numbers, such as suicide and rape hotlines. Create displays and hang up ALA's READ posters representing gay, lesbian, bisexual, and transgendered people. Generate booklists and Web lists of ALA's Gay/Lesbian Book Award and YALSA's awards that include books about GLBTQ teens. Promote the library and library resources. Set up a booth at gay pride day in your community. In Tucson, Arizona, library staff performed puppet shows about the Stonewall riots and the assassination of Harvey Milk at gay pride day. If there is a gay/straight alliance group in area high schools, consider promoting library materials to the group. If a youth group meets at a community center for gays and lesbians, consider attending a meeting to find out how the library can better serve this segment of the population.

Do not assume that everyone is straight and that all children and teenagers are being raised by a mother and a father. Become familiar with at-risk statistics relating to GLBTQ teens and learn how contact with others can help. Many GLBTQ teens are alienated from their families, suicidal, or abusers of drugs and alcohol. Some teen lesbians intentionally get pregnant to show that they are "normal." To establish a positive identity, GLBTQ teens need contact with other GLBTQ teens as well as positive adult role models. Create a safe environment for GLBTQ teens in the library, and set up sensitivity training sessions for staff members.

**Extreme Teen Tidbits: A Sampling of Library Web Pages
Featuring Booklists for Gay, Lesbian, Bisexual, Transgender,
and Questioning Teens**

- Berkeley (CA) Public Library
  http://www.berkeleypubliclibrary.org/teen/index.html

- Minneapolis (MN) Public Library
  http://www.mpls.lib.mn.us/wft/webforteens.asp

- Multnomah (OR) County Library
  http://www.multcolib.org/outer/index.html

- Plymouth (MI) District Library
  http://plymouthlibrary.org/glbt.htm

- San Francisco (CA) Public Library
  http://stpl.lib.ca.us/sfplonline/teen/booklists/glbteen2.htm

---

CONCLUSION

Welcoming extreme teens into your library and providing them with excellent service is not an easy goal, and it may take time to achieve. If your library is on the bottom rung, barely serving any teens in a positive way, it may take time and effort to move up the ladder. Extreme teens are at one end of the spectrum, and they require specialized services based on their unique needs. It is sometimes difficult to focus on serving one aspect of the community, but if the result is the loss of library users or potential library users, librarians should make an effort to serve the ex-

treme teen community incrementally, until the library can fully serve all
the different types of extreme teens.

WORKS CITED

Argetsinger, Amy. 1999. "Assembly Votes to Ban Some Teen Marriages."
Washington Post (April 11): C4.

Chelton, Mary K. 1994. **Excellence in Library Services to Young Adults: The Nation's Top Programs**. 1st ed. Chicago: American Library Association.

———. 1997. **Excellence in Library Services to Young Adults: The Nation's Top
Programs**. 2nd ed. Chicago: American Library Association.

———. 2000. **Excellence in Library Services to Young Adults: The Nation's Top
Programs**. 3rd ed. Chicago: American Library Association.

Deaver, Julie Reece. 1995. **Chicago Blues**. New York: HarperCollins.

Ferris, Jean. 1998. **Bad**. New York: Farrar, Straus and Giroux.

Flesch, Rudolf Franz. 1986. **Why Johnny Can't Read: And What You Can Do
About It**. New York: Harper and Row.

Garber, Marjorie. 1995. **Vice Versa: Bisexuality and the Eroticism of Everyday
Life**. New York: Simon and Schuster, 16.

Goldsmith, Francisca. 2002. "Earphone English." *School Library Journal* 48, issue 5
(May): 50–53.

Gross, Melissa. 1997. "Library Service to Pregnant Teens: How Can We Help?"
School Library Journal 43, issue 6 (June): 36.

Hainer, Michelle. 2004. "I'm 17 and I'm Getting Married." **Teen People** 7, issue 7,
(September): 182–184.

Hobbs, Valerie. 2004. **Letting Go of Bobby James, or How I Found Myself of
Steam**. New York: Farrar, Straus and Giroux.

Honawar, Vaishali. 2001. "Helping Homeless Students Learn." *Washington Times*
(February 22).

Hutchins, Loraine and Lani Kaahumana, ed. 1991. **Bi Any Other Name: Bisexual
People Speak Out**. New York: Alyson Books.

Judd, Alan. 2001. "Early-teen marriages investigated House of Prayer made Alabama wedding trips." *The Atlanta Constitution* (March 30): A1.

Levine, Judith. 2002. **Harmful to Minors: The Perils of Protecting Children from
Sex**. Minneapolis: University of Minnesota Press.

McGrath, Renee Vaillancourt. 2004. **Excellence in Library Services to Young Adults:
The Nation's Top Programs**. 4th ed. Chicago: American Library Association.

Myers, Walter Dean. 1999. **Monster**. New York: HarperCollins.

———. 2001. **Bad Boy: A Memoir**. New York: HarperCollins.

Reed, Shannon. 2004. "Legislature Should Pass House Bill 99." **Delaware State
News** (December 8): A5.

Rivera, Carla. 2002. "The State: Programs Help Train Young Fathers in Parenthood
and Cultural Heritage Services: The Lessons and Mentoring Are Directed

at Ethnic Groups That Often Lack Role Models in Their Own Upbringing."
Los Angeles Times (January 2): B6.

FOR FURTHER READING

Adams-Gordon, Beverly. 2000. **Home School, High School, and Beyond: A Time Management, Career Exploration, Organization, and Study Skills Course**. New York: Castlemoyle Books.

Angier, Naomi, and Katie O'Dell. 2001. "The Book Group Behind Bars." *Voice of Youth Advocates* (December): 331–333.

"Army Announces Programs to Boost Recruiting." 2000. *Army News Service*: Federal Document Clearinghouse, Inc. (February 3).

The Associated Press. 2002. "Married-Teens Numbers Rising" (November 9).

Ayer, Eleanor. 1997. **Everything You Need to Know about Teen Marriage**. New York: Rosen.

Barson, Michael, and Steven Heller. 1998. **Teenage Confidential: An Illustrated History of the American Teen**. San Francisco, CA: Chronicle Books.

Besharov, Douglas J., ed. 1999. **America's Disconnected Youth: Toward a Preventive Strategy**. Washington, DC: Child Welfare League of America.

Bolnick, Jamie. 2000. **Living at the Edge of the World: A Teenager's Survival in the Tunnels of Grand Central Station**. New York: St. Martin's Press.

Breuner, Cora Collette, Paul J. Barry, and Kathi J. Kemper. 1998. "Alternative Medicine Use by Homeless Youth." *Archives of Pediatrics and Adolescent Medicine* (November): 1071.

Bustos, Sergio. 2001. "Project Uses Volunteers to Foster Re-Enrollment." *Detroit News* (February 21).

Crouch, Michelle. 2001. "Debate: Some Too Young for Community Colleges?" *Charlotte Observer* (June 19).

Davis, Deborah, ed. 2004. **You Look Too Young to Be a Mom: Teen Mothers Speak Out on Love, Learning, and Success**. New York: Penguin.

Dembo, Richard, et al. "Urine Testing of Detained Juveniles to Identify High-Risk Youth." Justice Department, National Institute of Justice. SuDoc Number: J 28.24:Ur 3.

Draper, Sharon M. 1997. **Forged By Fire**. New York: Atheneum.

Dyrli, Odvard Egil. 1999. "Court Supports Teen Mothers for Honor Society." *Curriculum Administrator* 35, issue 3 (March): 6.

Edwards, Kirsten. 2002. **Teen Library Events: A Month-by-Month Guide**. Westport, CT: Greenwood Press.

Epps, Alice M. 1998. **Children Living in Temporary Shelters: How Homelessness Affects Their Perception of Home.** *Children of Poverty.* New York: Garland.

Falke, Joe. 1995. **Everything You Need to Know about Living in a Foster Home**. New York: Rosen.

Ferguson, Dawn B. 2000. "Getting Teens to Read." *Curriculum Administrator* 36, issue 9 (October): 21.

Foreman, Judy. 1999. "For Teenager, 'Confidential' Is Conditional." *Boston Globe* (January 18): D1.

Gibbons, Don C. 2002. "Juvenile Delinquency." **World Book Encyclopedia**.

Hartocollis, Anemona. 2001. "High School Dropout Rate Rises, and Levy Fears New Test Will Bring Huge Surge." *New York Times* (February 28): B6.

Hempelman, Kathleen A. 2000. **Teen Legal Rights**. Westport, CT: Greenwood Press.

Hombs, Mary Ellen. 2000. **American Homelessness: A Reference Handbook**. 3rd ed. Santa Barbara, CA: ABC-CLIO.

Honnold, RoseMary. 2003. **101+ Teen Programs That Work**. New York: Neal-Schuman.

Kurtzman, Laura. 1994. "Homeless Teens Get Posh Lunch." *Knight-Ridder News Service* (December 19).

Lindsay, Jeanne Warren. 1995. **Teenage Couples Coping with Reality: Dealing with Money, In-laws, Babies and Other Details of Daily Life**. Buena Park, CA: Morning Glory Press.

———. 1996. **Teenage Couples: Expectations and Reality: Teen Views on Living Together, Roles, Work, Jealousy, and Partner Abuse**. Buena Park, CA: Morning Glory Press.

———. 1997. **Books, Babies, and School-Age Parents: How to Teach Pregnant and Parenting Teens to Succeed**. Buena Park, CA: Morning Glory Press.

Maxym, Carol, and Leslie B. York. 2002. **Teens in Turmoil: A Path to Change for Parents, Adolescents, and Their Families**. New York: Viking.

McCaffery, Laura Hibbets. 1998. **Building an ESL Collection for Young Adults: A Bibliography of Recommended Fiction and Nonfiction for Schools and Public Libraries**. Westport, CT: Greenwood Press.

McCarthy, Carol Rohrer. 1999. "Dual-enrollment programs: Legislation Helps High School Students Enroll in College Courses." *Journal of Secondary Gifted Education* 11, issue 1 (Fall): 24–33.

McDaid, Farrah M. 2000. "Tribal Teen Pregnancies Raise Red Flag." *California Journal* (May): 18–21.

Mundowney, JoAnn G. 2001. **Hold Them in Your Heart: Successful Strategies for Library Services to At-Risk Teens**. New York: Neal-Schuman.

New Jersey State Library. 2002. "Guidelines for Young Adult Services in Public Libraries of New Jersey" (Spring).

Nichols, Janet. 1999. "Building Bridges: High School and University Partnerships for Information Literacy." *NASSP Bulletin* 83, no. 605 (March): 75–81.

Peterson, Virginia. 2001. **Homeless: Struggling to Survive**. New York: Gale Group.

Rion, David. 2000. "National Guard Program Aids Troubled Youth." *Army Link News* (July 18).

Rubin, Jeffrey. 2000. "Don't Try It at Home." *Scholastic Action* 23, issue 11 (March 6): 4–6.

Sells, Scott P. 1998. **Treating the Tough Adolescent: A Family-Based, Step-by-Step Guide**. New York: Guilford Press.

Shapiro, Joseph P. 1995. "Sins of the Fathers: It Is Adult Males Who Are Fathering the Babies Born to Teenagers." *U.S. News and World Report* (August 14): 51–52.

Sparks, Beatrice. 1996. **Almost Lost: The True Story of an Anonymous Teenager's Life on the Streets**. New York: Avon.

Stasio, Frank. 2001. "Profile: New Study Suggests High Dropout Rates May Be Concentrated in 300 Schools in the Inner Cities of America." *National Public Radio* (January 14).

Stewart, Gail B. 1999. **Homeless Teens**. San Diego, CA: Lucent Books.

Tauber, Michelle. 2002. "Playing for Keeps." *People* 57, issue 15 (April 22): 92–99.

Thomas, Jack. 2004. "Hope For the Future: With the Right to Marry in the Balance, Gay Teens Dream of a Wedding Day." *Boston Globe* (January 20): E1.

3

EXTREME RESOURCES: BUILDING COLLECTIONS

Imagine that you are at a high school reunion. Not a typical reunion where you cannot remember the name of that guy who used to be attractive but is now bald and has a beer belly, but one made up of more familiar people—extreme teens from young adult literature. Those who wreaked havoc or overcame some difficult feat in the pages of your favorite book are now gathered around you, sipping drinks and remembering way back when. Now, think about the multitude of resources that are available today in libraries. There are nonfiction series that tackle social issues specifically for teens. There are links to helpful organizations from library Web pages. Computer-savvy teens are likely to use the Internet to gather information about their problems. If these resources had been accessible in the past, perhaps these extreme teens would have had an easier time coping with their situations.

Would July and Bo Jo Jones (Head 1967) have had an easier time raising a child if they had access to books, videos, games, and organizations specifically for teen parents? Would orphaned Ponyboy Curtis and his brothers (Hinton 1967) have had less turmoil in their lives if they had consulted library books on gangs and independent living? Instead of using her father's encyclopedia for information and being disappointed by what she read, Liza Winthrop (Garden 1982) might have consulted a vast amount of print and online materials relating to homosexuality in a library staffed with—in a perfect library world—caring and nonjudgmental adults who have been properly trained. Let us consider library collections that address the issues relating to the lives of extreme teens.

DETERMINING POLICIES AND YOUR AUDIENCE

When building a library collection, the place to start is by consulting your library's materials selection policy. Some libraries have one policy for the entire library, while larger libraries may have different policies for various departments, depending on the clientele and their information needs. For example, in the same public library, a genealogy department might focus on research materials, whereas a youth services department might purchase materials that are both recreational and informational.

Determine your audience when building a library collection. Use local demographic information to help decide what to purchase. Do your teen patrons speak English fluently? Is it necessary to devote a large portion of the collection development budget to ESL materials? Is there a high teen pregnancy rate in your area, or is it likely that many teens have taken abstinence pledges in your community? Are there many teens homeschooled in the area? These are just some of the questions to consider as you create a library collection that will be useful to your patrons.

In addition to relying on standard collection development tools, such as *Voice of Youth Advocates*, *Booklist*, and *School Library Journal*, go online to determine what teens are interested in and what types of materials they like to listen to, read, and watch. Sites like amazon.com are useful in determining the reactions of teens to books and other materials. Also, pay attention to efforts by professional library organizations in getting the word out about teen reading. YALSA's Teen's Top Ten allows the members of Teen Advisory Groups throughout the country to vote for their favorite books.

Strive for balance and diversity in your collection, in both fiction and nonfiction. Purchase novels that feature extreme teens, as well as informational sources that meet their needs. Last but definitely not least, talk to teens! Not only those who are in the library, but those who hang out outside of the library, those to whom you are related, and those who may be volunteers or library employees. With extreme teens, you might need to step out of your building to seek your audience. In a juvenile detention center, you can talk to teens about what they want the library to offer. Immigrant teens may offer a lot of insight into creating a more multicultural collection. Visit local bookstores and see what peaks teens' interests.

As with any library collection (besides those that specifically focus on historical documents), it is important to make sure that the materials are current. A legal book for teens that gives advice about becoming emancipated, copyright 1990, has little value in the year 2005. Medical and psychology books stating that gay males are mentally ill should not be on your shelves if you are trying to maintain an accurate and up-to-date collection. Homeschooling practices have changed over the years, and it is necessary for libraries to stay current with educational trends.

Another issue relating to currency is the condition and appeal of book covers. Keeping ratty-looking books, especially paperbacks, is counterproductive because teens and other library patrons are typically reluctant to check out books that look as though Fido has been chewing on them. Always buy the most recent edition of a book, preferably a paperback, with a catchy new cover, instead of relying on the old stuff. Teens are hypersensitive to how things look and they will be more likely to check out a book with an eye-catching cover instead of a hardbound book jacket with dated-looking characters on the front.

Diversity is the key when building collections for extreme teens, not only in the types of materials, but also in reading levels and format. While a dual-enrollment student may be reading all of Shakespeare's plays, a high school dropout may be struggling to keep up with a children's chapter book in tandem with the same story told in the format of a recorded book. Although the library may have an abundance of books about homelessness, the homeless teen may feel more comfortable accessing a Web site about the subject.

Words about Weeding

Just like the seasons, the collection development process is cyclical. In the spring, you may be blessed with a large collection development budget. And lots of rain. In the fall, though, the budget, as well as the leaves, may dry up. The summer months may be a time in your library when staff members concentrate on weeding. In the winter, library managers might evaluate the collection and determine strengths and weaknesses for future budget allocations.

Extreme teens need current information about laws that pertain to them, health, and other time-sensitive issues. Outdated information about child care is hardly useful. On the other hand, the copyright date is not the only criteria by which to judge a book's worth. And just because an item has a low rate of circulation does not mean it is not being used within the library. Novels such as *The Catcher in the Rye* and *The Outsiders* were published decades ago, but they are still read and enjoyed by today's teen readers. Extreme teens may be too embarrassed or scared to check out certain materials. Books about certain topics may be regularly stolen or go missing, later to be found dog-eared and put back on the wrong shelf. Although it may seem like throwing money away, it is important to continue purchasing popular items for extreme teens, even though they do not last forever.

FICTION

Many adolescents who are worried about matters they hesitate to discuss find what they are looking for in teen-age stories. Most of these are adequately written; they are neither pornographic or Communistic, they hurt no one, and they afford a great deal of pleasure to a lot of young people. (Edwards, 1969, 82–83)

Works of fiction can serve different purposes for extreme teens. Teens may use realistic fiction (sometimes called "issues fiction" or "problem novels") as a type of bibliotherapy to cope with their lives. This is fiction that they can relate to and that mirrors their lives—it validates their experiences and identity and may even offer insights into and solutions to their problems. Other extreme teens may prefer to read science fiction and fantasy works in order to escape from the harsh reality of their lives. Realistic fiction, whether for adults or teens, can be useful to help teens sort through their problems and explore possible solutions. Typically, realistic fiction portrays life as accurately as possible. Parents, librarians, and other youth service workers should become familiar with realistic fiction, especially if they can assist extreme teens to understand and cope with their problems.

Extreme Teen Tidbits: Chronology of Benchmark Novels about Nontraditional Teens

- 1951 *The Catcher in the Rye* by J.D. Salinger. After being expelled from boarding school, Holden Caulfield travels to New York and encounters tourists, a prostitute, a former classmate, and a former teacher before visiting his sister and avoiding his parents.

- 1967 *Mr. and Mr. Bo Jo Jones* by Ann Head. Sixteen-year-old July and seventeen-year-old Bo Jo decide to get married when they discover that they are going to become parents.

- 1974 *If Beale Street Could Talk* by James Baldwin. Fonny finds himself unjustly arrested but his pregnant girlfriend Tish is determined to help him.

- 1975 *Rumble Fish* by S. E. Hinton. Rusty-James and his brother find it difficult to live among gang activity.

- 1982 *Annie on My Mind* by Nancy Garden. Liza, a college student, reminisces about her previous relationship with Annie.

- 1982 *Dance on My Grave* by Aidan Chambers. Hal's summer affair with Barry Gorman ends tragically when Hal discovers he is much more committed to the relationship than his friend.

- 1987 *The Crazy Horse Electric Game* by Chris Crutcher. A high school athlete, frustrated at being handicapped after an accident, runs away from home and is helped back to mental and physical health by people in a special school.

- 1993 *Make Lemonade* by Virginia Euwer Wolff. In order to earn money for college, fourteen-year-old LaVaughn babysits for a teenage mother.

- 1994 *Too Soon for Jeff* by Marilyn Reynolds. Upset when he learns that his girlfriend is pregnant and determined not to let a baby ruin his plans to go to college on a debate scholarship, high school senior Jeff Browning finds that his feelings have change after the baby is born.

Extreme Teen Tidbits: Insightful Quotations from Teen Literature

- *Beginner's Luck: A Novel*, by Laura Pedersen. "My project at the library is to verify that the legal age to quit school and work full-time is sixteen and to find out at what age you can divorce your parents, if it's even possible, in the state of Ohio." (p. 80)

- *The Body of Christopher Creed* by Carol Plum-Ucci. "Bo quit school when she did, figuring he had no reason to go anymore; he was almost eighteen, anyway. He took a job at a gas station" (p. 315)

- *Can't Get There From Here* by Todd Strasser. "Did they discover life on another planet? I never wondered for long because then I'd get hungry and have to look for something to eat. Or I got cold or I needed money. I guess that's why homeless kids don't go to school. They're too busy just trying to stay alive." (p. 127)

- *The First Part Last* by Angela Johnson. "I can hardly keep my eyes open in Brit Lit. I got so much drool on my arm I can't even try to wipe it on my shirt. I seriously need a tissue or a paper towel. I was up all night with Feather, who thinks two in the morning is party time." (p. 41)

- *The Last Chance Texaco* by Brent Hartinger. "That afternoon, I was alone in my bedroom reading when someone knocked on the door. I long since learned that counselors got suspicious whenever they saw a kid doing something really unusual, like reading a novel, so I slipped the book under my bedspread." (p. 36)

- *Mary Wolf: A Novel* by Cynthia D. Grant. "My parents don't like problems, don't like coming to school for meetings. There are too many questions they can't answer. They're ashamed to explain that we live in our RV. In big cities there are lots of homeless people, but in little towns you feel like a freak." (p. 30)

- *The Maze* by Will Hobbs. "The library was intolerably boring unless you were actually going to read. And guys who liked to read weren't the kind looking for trouble." (p. 8)

- *Playing without the Ball: A Novel in Four Quarters* by Rich Wallace. "I get rent free. Not exactly free—I work it off in Shorty's kitchen three or four nights a week. The deal includes meals during work hours and five dollars an hour off the books." (p. 4)

- *Rainbow High* by Alex Sanchez. "Every day I have to deal with homophobia. And yet in classes, sex hardly ever gets addressed, especially homosexuality, as if it doesn't exist." (p. 237)

- *Shooter* by Walter Dean Myers. "Sergeant Razor Sharp said I looked like a Fine Young Man and I said he looked like a Fine Young Man and he said 'You are a smart Fine Young Man' and we sat down and went over my Military Options." (pp. 210–211)

NONFICTION

Nonfiction for teens has often gotten short shrift in library collections, but that is changing as so many more publishers produce nonfiction materials for this age group. Extreme teens need a strong nonfiction collection that fulfills their informational needs. Homeschooled teens may rely heavily on the public library's collection for curricular support. Parents who decide to homeschool their teens will need general information about homeschooling laws, high school graduation requirements, GED requirements, and creating a curriculum that is comparable to a regular high school curriculum. Homeschooled teens who are college bound and are without the assistance of a guidance counselor or school library collection require information about scholarships, financial aid, college requirements, and majors. Homeschooled students often need information about participation in extracurricular activities, such as involvement with the Scouts, 4-H clubs, community service, youth sports, or employment. Like traditional high school students, they also need information about taking standardized tests as well as how best to study for them.

Librarians serving teens in dual-enrollment programs, in which they attend college as well as high school, can partner with local colleges when building their collections. Students sometimes request the resources of the public library as well as those at colleges.

High school dropouts typically need GED study guides and books that cover basic skills. Also, consider creating a collection of books about high school dropouts so that potential dropouts can read about what life may be like if they drop out of school.

Teens who are emancipated from their parents often need information about consumer health, laws in relation to tenants' rights and landlords' responsibilities, time management, budgeting, finance, household repairs, grocery shopping, cooking, nutrition, laundry, ironing, and cleaning.

Married teenagers and those planning to marry can benefit from information about successful marriages and other topics that concern marriage, such as planning a wedding, laws, sexuality, maintaining healthy relationships, and, at the other end of the spectrum, spousal abuse. Since divorce rates are high among people who marry when they are still teenagers, this is also an important topic for teens who plan to marry.

Pregnant and parenting teens need books about nonfiction topics including legal issues relating to parenting, custody and child support, adoption, abortion, abortion alternatives, breastfeeding, discipline, caring for infants and children, financial issues, and prenatal care.

Teens engaged in any type of sexual activity need accurate and up-to-date information about sexuality. Incarcerated teens and juvenile delinquents often seek nonfiction works relating to laws and employment.

SPECIAL CONSIDERATIONS IN PROVIDING MATERIALS ABOUT GLBTQ ISSUES

Be aware that some teens who question their sexuality may be hesitant to approach the sections in a library or a bookstore that are set up specifically for those who are gay, lesbian, bisexual, transgender, or questioning. Others may be completely comfortable in those sections of the library or bookstore. In your library it is important to represent diverse groups of people throughout the entire library collection. Be prepared to encounter members of the public, coworkers, library administrators, or politicians who question why it is necessary to include materials about GLBTQ issues for teens. You may be faced with the opinion that GLBTQ teens do not live in your community. A response to this sentiment might be, "Have you asked every person in your community?" Others may firmly state that they disapprove of homosexuality and materials about the subject being available for teens. Consider responding that personal prejudices cannot impact other library users who may wish to access these materials. You may want to gently remind those who complain that unless they are the parents or legal guardians of the minor accessing the information, they have no legal control over the situation.

Dewey Know Dewey?

Below are suggested topics within the different ranges of the Dewey Decimal System that represent diverse topics in sexual identity:

000: gay-oriented reference books; books about serving GLBTQ teens in libraries

200: the relationship between sexual identity and spirituality

300: legal rights, marriage, and "coming out" books

600: sex and health education

700: gay topics in films, music, and photography

800: literature written by and about GLBTQ teens

900: history of gays and biographies

BOOKLISTS, PAMPHLETS, AND MAGAZINES

Consider purchasing or creating booklists and pamphlets that can be placed in the library for teens who have questions that they may be too embarrassed to ask the library staff. Many organizations produce brochures that offer current information on topics such as drugs, violence, peer pressure, sexuality, and depression. Place these materials in strategic locations where teens can view them without library staff seeing them. Teens will be more likely to pick up the materials if they do not feel they are being watched.

For a more local focus, create your own pamphlets, booklists, or bookmarks and include information about library resources and local organizations or hotlines related to timely topics based on specific community needs.

Magazines are not evil pieces of paper stuck together with lots of photographs that keep teens from reading! If a teen opens a magazine, reading happens. Adults, even librarians, tend to view reading magazines as not really reading at all. This is far from the truth. A strong library collection for any teenager, extreme or not, includes a vast assortment of magazines. Many teens are likely to pick up standard magazines, produced for teens and adults, offered in libraries. Magazines that are popular with teens include those that are produced specifically for them, such as *Seventeen* and *Teen People*, as well as many adult magazines about a variety of topics including cars, sports, hobbies, news, and bridal magazines. Some magazines have stood the test of time, such as *Mad*, which offers humor related to current events. Thinking outside the library, it is likely that teens in juvenile detention centers would also enjoy having access to an array of magazines.

BEYOND BOOKS: ONLINE RESOURCES, VIDEOS, DVDs, AUDIOBOOKS, AND SOFTWARE

Books and other printed materials should not be the only resources that your library has available for extreme teens, especially in this age of wireless networks and PDAs. Videos and DVDs offer ways to learn about subjects that may be more gratifying to some teens, especially those who have difficulty reading. Distributors are beginning to offer more titles on DVD, the preferred format for many teens and librarians who do not wish to continue buying a format that is quickly going out of date.

Recorded books, on both cassette and compact disc, are especially useful for teens who are learning English as a second language, reluctant readers, and dual-enrollment students. Teens learning English and reluctant readers may find it easier to listen to a recorded book instead of reading it, or combining the two for a better experience overall. Teens can sit at the back of a school bus and listen to a book, and their friends will not know that they are listening to a book instead of the latest top musician. Those whose job it is to read audiobooks are often skilled performers, and listening to someone read is an entirely different experience. Good performers can use different accents and create a theatrical performance for the listener. Teens attending both high school and college may be extremely busy, and if they can access recorded books, and, for instance, listen to them while traveling from high school to college, they can both learn and use their time effectively.

Do not assume that all teens have computer access at home or at school. Some extreme teens may not be attending school; others may not even have a place to call home. Extreme teens may need assistance in finding online information that is current and accurate. To promote useful and authentic Web sites, consider adding links from your library's Web page to those organizations that focus on services to extreme teens. Invest in electronic databases that are strong in the area of teen issues, such as SIRS Knowledge Source, which features topic-based research with articles from hundreds of newspapers and magazines. Extreme teens will find an array of information through electronic databases such as EBSCO Masterfile and the Gale Junior Reference Collection. Teens who may be reluctant readers, but enjoy using computers, may find that World Book Online or the New Book of Knowledge online are better alternatives to printed resources. Another useful database for extreme teens is LearningExpressLibrary, which offers test study guides in cosmetology, advanced placement courses, GED, high school skills improvement, the military, reading skills improvement, Test of English as a Foreign Language (TOEFL), U.S. citizenship, writing skills improvement, skills improvement in Spanish, and more.

Even though the printed word has historically been at the heart of librarianship, some ideas and concepts improve when projected through hearing and visual aids. For reluctant readers, a recorded book may be just the thing to encourage them to graduate from high school instead of dropping out. Video clips of historical footage, perhaps of hate crimes, may be helpful in keeping juvenile delinquents from repeating their behavior. Computer software can be used to simulate situations that extreme teens may face in the future, such as interactive multimedia products that allow pregnant teens to virtually experience and prepare for the imminent birth of their babies. It is important to accept that nonprint resources are useful, especially if you are working with teenagers who may not know how to read—or may not know how to read anything in English.

SUGGESTED RESOURCES

The following list of books, magazines, videos, DVDs, organizations, Web sites, and yes, even board games, are good choices for those ages twelve through nineteen who may be considered nontraditional. Not all of the materials listed are produced specifically for young adults. Most of the annotations were derived from the Library of Congress. The lists can be used to help build your collection, form readers' advisory groups, create booklists, and share with parents, youth service workers, and other librarians.

Please keep in mind that just because the materials reflect the lives of nontraditional teens does not mean that all extreme teens will be interested in reading these materials. Like any other teenager, extreme teens have varied reading interests representing a full range of topics and genres.

Fiction about Incarceration

Flinn, Alex. 2001. **Breathing Underwater**. New York: HarperCollins. Sent to counseling for hitting his girlfriend Caitlin, and ordered to keep a journal, Nick, age sixteen, recounts his relationship with her, examines his controlling behavior and anger, and describes living with his abusive father.

Karr, Kathleen. 2000. **The Boxer**. New York: Farrar, Straus and Giroux. Having learned how to box while in prison, fifteen-year-old Johnny sets out to discover if he can make a decent living as a fighter in late-nineteenth-century New York City.

Fiction about Violence and Delinquency

Cadnum, Michael. 2000. **Redhanded**. New York: Viking. Since he cannot depend on his father, Stephen feels as though his only chance to make it to the big boxing tournament is to go along with the dangerous plan of a local tough guy to whom he has been introduced by a thrill-seeking friend.

Coburn, Jake. 2003. **Prep**. New York: Dutton. A one-time tag artist, Nick tries to come to terms with the death of a friend, protect the brother of his would-be girlfriend, escape the violence of wealthy New York City prep-school hoods, and figure out who he really is.

Coleman, Michael. 2004. **On the Run**. New York: Dutton. When a persistent youth offender is caught yet again, he is sentenced to community service as the partner to a blind runner.

Dessen, Sarah. 2000. **Dreamland: A Novel**. New York: Viking. After her older sister runs away, Caitlin, age sixteen, decides that she needs to make a major change in her own life and enters into an abusive relationship with a boy who is mysterious, brilliant, and dangerous.

Draper, Sharon. 2003. **Battle of Jericho**. New York: Simon and Schuster. Jericho, age sixteen, finds that life is becoming more difficult as a result of his decision to pledge for the Warriors of Distinction, one of the most exclusive gangs in school.

Heynen, Jim. 2000. **Cosmos Coyote and William the Nice**. New York: HarperTempest. When sent to live on a farm in Iowa as an alternative to juvenile detention, Cosmos, age seventeen, falls in love with a religious girl and reconsiders his values and beliefs.

Jones, Patrick. 2004. **Things Change**. New York: Walker and Co. Joanna, age sixteen, one of the best students in her class, develops a passionate attachment for Paul, age seventeen, who is deeply troubled.

Mikaelsen, Ben. 2001. **Touching Spirit Bear**. New York: HarperCollins. After his anger erupts into violence, Cole, to avoid going to prison, agrees to participate in a sentencing alternative.

Myers, Walter Dean. 2002. **Handbook for Boys: A Novel**. New York: HarperCollins. On probation for assault, sixteen-year-old Jimmy talks about life with three senior citizens in a Harlem barbershop and hears about the tools he can use to succeed in life.

———. 2004. **Shooter**. New York: HarperCollins. Written in the form of interviews, reports, and journal entries, the story of three troubled teenagers ends in a tragic school shooting.

Pierre, D.B.C. 2003. **Vernon God Little**. New York: Canongate Books. In the town of Martirio, Texas, fifteen-year-old Vernon Little is in trouble. His friend, Jesus, has just killed sixteen of his classmates before turning the gun on himself.

Sebold, Alice. 2002. **The Lovely Bones: A Novel.** Boston: Little, Brown. Susie, age fourteen, speaks from heaven after being brutally raped and murdered.

Strasser, Todd. 2000. **Give a Boy a Gun**. New York: Simon and Schuster. Gary and Brendan hold their classmates hostage at a Middletown High School dance.

Watt, Alan. 2000. **Diamond Dogs**. Boston: Little, Brown. Neil Garvin, age seventeen, the quarterback of the high school football team, accidentally commits a terrible crime.

Nonfiction about Delinquency, Incarceration, and Violence

Canfield, Jack, ed. 2000. **Chicken Soup for the Prisoner's Soul: 101 Stories to Open the Heart and Rekindle the Spirit of Hope, Healing and Forgiveness**. Deerfield Beach, FL: Health Communications. This book includes stories about prisoners and their families. The stories are categorized by topic, such as family, change, faith, forgiveness, kindness, love, wisdom, and overcoming obstacles. The writers include inmates, former inmates, educators, parents, ministers, social workers, correctional officers, professional speakers, cartoonists, and more.

Kuklin, Susan. 2001. **Trial: The Inside Story**. New York: Henry Holt. The author followed a criminal trial for kidnapping from beginning to end and reports on her observations. Interspersed with photographs, court transcripts, interviews, and sidebars of information, this book is an excellent introduction to the justice system. The work includes a glossary of law terms, a thorough index, and suggestions for further reading.

Marzilli, Alan. 2003. **Famous Crimes of the 20th Century**. Philadelphia: Chelsea House. This work describes some of the major crimes committed in the United States during the twentieth century and discusses the social impact of these criminal acts and the trials and punishments of the perpetrators.

Orr, Tamra. 2003. **Violence in Our Schools: Halls of Hope, Halls of Fear**. Danbury, CT: Franklin Watts. Chronicles school violence and discusses its causes, perpetrators, and solutions. Includes "Questions to Ponder" and specific advice for individual action.

Roleff, Tamara L., ed. 2000. **Crime and Criminals: Opposing Viewpoints**. San Diego, CA: Greenhaven Press. This edited collection of essays includes topics that are pertinent to nontraditional teens, including whether juveniles should be treated as adults, information about gun control, how the media focuses on troubled teens, and whether imposing civil ordinances against gangs is unconstitutional. The book includes a detailed list of organizations to contact for more information, a book and periodical bibliography, and questions for further discussion.

Weill, Sabrina Solin. 2002. **We're Not Monsters: Teens Speak Out About Teens in Trouble**. New York: HarperCollins. Interspersed with statistics and comments from teenagers about crime, this book focuses on specific crimes committed by youth.

DVDs and Videos about Delinquency, Incarceration, and Violence

In the Mix: Live by the Gun, Die by the Gun. 1998. 29 minutes. DVD and video. New York: Castle Works Inc. The In The Mix series, produced by PBS, features timely topics for teens. In this documentary, teens who have been affected by guns are interviewed, including former gang members, teen gun owners, and friends of gunshot victims.

In the Mix: School Violence: Answers from the Inside. 1998. 30 minutes. DVD and video. New York: Castle Works Inc. Features students at a diverse suburban high school and how they interact with various cliques.

Invisible Revolution: A Youth Subculture of Hate. 2000. 55 minutes. Video. New York: Filmakers Library. Features youth who are members of a white supremacy group and also a group calling themselves the Anti-Racist Action (ARA).

Once a Criminal Always a Criminal: Can Youth Offenders Rehabilitate Themselves? 2001. 19 minutes. Video. New York: Educational Video Center. This documentary features the lives of Ariel and Andre, who have spent time in prison but are trying to improve their lives through the Friends of Rikers Island program.

Teen Files: The Truth about Violence. 2000. 90 minutes. DVD and video. Chatsworth, CA: AIMS Multimedia. Explores violence and its consequences through the eyes of teens from Los Angeles.

Tough on Crime, Tough on Our Kind. 2000. 30 minutes. Video. New York: Educational Video Center. This examination of the New York City juvenile justice system includes personal stories of incarcerated youth and interviews with social workers, lawyers, and others who interact with young criminals.

Organizations and Online Resources about Delinquency, Incarceration, and Violence

National Youth Gang Center (NYGC)
http://www.iir.com/nygc

Office of Justice Programs (OJP)
http://www.ojp.usdoj.gov

Office of Juvenile Justice and Delinquency Prevention (OJJDP)
http://ojjdp.ncjrs.org

Youth Crime Watch of America
9300 South Dadeland Boulevard
Suite 100

Miami, FL 33156
(305) 670-2409

Fiction about Dropouts

Halliday, John. 2003. **Shooting Monarchs**. New York: McElderry Books. Macy and
   Danny, two teenage boys who have both grown up under difficult circumstances, turn out very differently.
McDonald, Janet. 2003. **Spellbound**. New York: Frances Foster Books. Raven, a
   teenage mother and high school dropout living in a housing project, decides, with the help and sometime interference of her best friend Aisha, to
   study for a spelling bee that could lead to a college preparatory program
   and four-year scholarship.
McDonell, Nick. 2002. **Twelve**. New York: Grove Press. Mike, age seventeen, a
   high school dropout, sells drugs to affluent teenagers in Manhattan.
Prete, David. 2003. **Say That to My Face**. New York: Norton. Desperate to escape
   the apathy and violence of Yonkers, Joe Frascone, an idealistic Italian
   American young man, searches for a way to overcome his broken heart and
   fractured family to seek his dreams in New York City.

Fiction about Emancipated Teens

Pedersen, Laura. 2003. **Beginner's Luck: A Novel**. New York: Ballantine. Hallie
   Palmer, age sixteen, an avid gambler and the second of seven children,
   quits school, runs away from home, and becomes a yard person for Mrs.
   Olivia Stockton and her eccentric family.
Wallace, Rich. 2000. **Playing Without the Ball: A Novel in Four Quarters**. New
   York: Alfred A. Knopf. Abandoned by his parents, who have gone their
   separate ways and left him behind in a small Pennsylvania town, Jay, age
   seventeen, finds hope for the future in a church-sponsored basketball team
   and a female friend.

Nonfiction about Emancipated Teens

Dudevszky, Szabinka. 1999. **Close-Up**. Asheville, NC: Front Street Press. Features
   young people who cannot live with their parents for various reasons.

Fiction about Teens in Foster Care

Cann, Katie. 2004. **Shacked Up**. New York: Simon Pulse. Living the good life with
   a fancy, free apartment and a great job, Rich is happy with the way things
   are going and feels confident about his chances with the beautiful Portia,
   but when his old friend Bonny is in need of a place to stay, Rich cannot refuse her.

Fleischman, Paul. 2003. **Breakout**. Chicago: Cricket Books. A young woman presents a play based on her life as a seventeen-year-old runaway whose escape from her foster home in Los Angeles is thwarted by an all-day traffic jam, an event that provides time for her to explore her free-floating identity, hunger for her unknown mother, and yearning for human connection.

Giff, Patricia Reilly. 2002. **Pictures of Hollis Woods**. New York: Dell Yearling Book. A troublesome twelve-year-old orphan, staying with an elderly artist who needs her, remembers the only other time she was happy in a foster home, with a family that truly seemed to care about her.

Harris, Mete Ivie. 2003. **The Monster in Me**. New York: Holiday House. In a small town near Salt Lake City, Utah, a caring foster family and a love of running help thirteen-year-old Natalie Wills feel that she can have a normal life, despite having been raised by a drug-addicted mother.

Hartinger, Brent. 2004. **Last Chance Texaco**. New York: HarperTempest. Troubled teen Lucy Pitt struggles to fit in as a tenant at a last-chance foster home.

Hubler, Marsha. 2004. **A True Test for Skye**. Grand Rapids, MI: Zonderkidz. The love of her foster parents, her friend Morgan, and her own devotion to the horses and dogs at Keystone Stables help Skye become a Christian and find a way to help her troubled friend Sooze.

Woodson, Jacqueline. 2003. **Locomotion**. New York: G. P. Putnam's Sons. In a series of poems, eleven-year-old Lonnie writes about his life after the death of his parents. He is separated from his younger sister and lives in a foster home, but finds his poetic voice at school.

Videos about Teens in Foster Care

Not Me, Not Mine: Adult Survivors of Foster Care. 2003. 30 minutes. Video. New York: Educational Video Center. This documentary features seven foster care youth who originally appeared in a production called *Someplace to Call Home*. The adult survivors of the foster care system discuss the challenges they have faced after being part of the foster care system.

Someplace to Call Home: Surviving the Foster Care System. 1995. 30 minutes. New York: Educational Video Center. This video gives advice to foster care youth regarding their rights and reveals what life is like for teens living in foster care and group homes.

Organizations and Online Resources about Foster Care

National Adoption Information Clearinghouse
http://naic.acf.hhs.gov

National Resource Center for Foster Care and Permanency Planning
http://www.hunter.cuny.edu/socwork/nrcfcpp

National Resource Center for Special Needs Adoption
http://www.nrcadoption.org

Fiction about Married Teens

Clarke, Kathryn Ann. 2004. **The Breakable Vow**. New York: Avon. After Annie, age eighteen, becomes unexpectedly pregnant, she marries her boyfriend, but slowly realizes that he is abusive and that she must decide what she can and will do about the relationship to keep her daughter safe. Includes information on the characteristics of abusive relationships and how to end them.

Hobbs, Valerie. 2004. **Letting Go of Bobby James, or How I Found My Self of Steam**. New York: Farrar, Straus and Giroux. After being left by her husband at a gas station in Florida, sixteen-year-old Sally Jo Walker, also known as Jody, wants a better life for herself and makes some difficult decisions.

Krulik, Nancy. 2005. **Newly Wed**. New York: Simon Pulse. This book follows a year in the life of a wedded couple who meet online.

Sparks, Nicholas. 2000. **A Walk to Remember**. New York: Warner Books. Set in North Carolina in 1948, this tale involves Jamie and Landon, a married teenage couple.

Fiction about Homelessness

Berger, John. 1999. **King: A Street Story**. New York: Pantheon. King, a dog, tells the story of the life and conditions of the people with whom he lives in a squatter's community in Saint Valry, France.

Brooks, Martha. 2000. **Being with Henry**. New York: DK. After his mother and new stepfather throw Laker out of the house, the homeless teen befriends eighty-three-year-old Henry.

Carey, Janet Lee. 2004. **The Double-Life of Zoe Flynn**. New York: Simon and Schuster. When Zoe's father loses his job, her family begins living out of a van, and she lies to teachers and friends to keep the family's secret.

Collier, James Lincoln. 2001. **Chipper**. New York: Marshall Cavendish. Chipper, age twelve, is an orphaned, homeless member of a street-wise gang in 1890s New York City.

Easton, Kelly. 2004. **Walking on Air**. New York: Margaret K. McElderry Books. In 1931, a young girl travels around the country performing on a tightrope during revival meetings held by her father and seeks her own answers about God, her family, and her life of poverty and homelessness.

Koja, Kate. 2004. **The Blue Mirror**. New York: Farrar, Straus and Giroux. Maggy Klass, age seventeen, who frequently seeks refuge from her alcoholic mother's apartment by sitting and drawing in a local café, becomes involved in a destructive relationship with a charismatic homeless youth named Cole.

Strasser, Todd. 2004. **Can't Get There from Here**. New York: Simon and Schuster. Tired of being hungry, cold, and dirty from living on the streets of New York City with a tribe of other homeless teenagers who are dying one by one, a girl named Maybe ponders her future and longs for someone to care about her.

Fiction about Runaways

Clark, Robert. 2002. **Love Among the Ruins: A Novel**. New York: Vintage Books. In the summer of 1968, two teenagers become lovers and run away to create a new life in the wilderness.

Herrick, Steven. 2004. **The Simple Gift**. New York: Simon and Schuster. Billy, age sixteen, hits the road and looks for a new life after he determines that he can no longer deal with his alcoholic, abusive father.

Moriarty, Jaclyn. 2000. **Feeling Sorry for Celia**. New York: St. Martin's Press. Elizabeth Clarry's best friend has run away again, her absent father has reappeared, and her dialogue with her mother consists of notes left on the fridge.

Napoli, Donna Jo. 2004. **North**. New York: Greenwillow Books. Tired of his mother's overprotectiveness and intrigued by the life of African American explorer Matthew Henson, twelve-year-old Alvin travels north and spends a season with a trapper near the Arctic Circle.

Plum-Ucci, Carol. **The Body of Christopher Creed**. New York: Harcourt. When Christopher Creed, the class weirdo, disappears without a trace, fellow students and citizens of Steepleton speculate about what happened to him.

Rapp, Adam. 2003. **33 Snowfish**. Cambridge, MA: Candlewick Press. A homeless boy, running from the police with a drug-addicted prostitute, gets the chance to make a better life for himself.

Rottman, S. L. 2003. **Shadow of a Doubt**. Atlanta, GA: Peachtree. As his sophomore year in high school begins, fifteen-year-old Shadow joins the forensics team, makes new friends, and struggles to cope with the return of his older brother, who ran away seven years earlier and now faces a murder trial.

Sumner, Melanie. 2001. **The School of Beauty and Charm: A Novel**. Chapel Hill, NC: Algonquin Books of Chapel Hill. Louise, age eighteen, runs off to join a carnival after struggling to fit in with her family in Georgia.

Whelan, Gloria. 2004. **Chu Ju's House**. New York: HarperCollins. In order to save her baby sister, Chu Ju, age fourteen, leaves her rural home in modern China and earns food and shelter by working on a fishing boat, tending silk worms, and planting rice seedlings, while wondering if she will ever see her family again.

Wyss, Thelma Hatch. 2002. **Ten Miles from Winnemucca**. New York: Harper-
Collins. When his mother and her new husband take off on a long honey-
moon and his new stepbrother throws his belongings out the window,
Martin, age sixteen, takes off in his Jeep and settles in Red Rock, Idaho,
where he finds a job, enrolls in school, and suffers from loneliness.

Nonfiction about Homelessness and Runaways

Bolnick, Tina S. and Jamie Pastor. 2000. **Living at the Edge of the World: A
Teenager's Survival in the Tunnels of Grand Central Station**. New York:
St. Martin's Press. Tina's story of surviving in the tunnels among drugs,
crime, and violence.
Paulsen, Gary. 2000. **The Beet Fields: A Sixteenth Summer**. New York: Delacorte.
The author recalls his experiences as a migrant laborer and carnival worker
after he ran away from home at age sixteen.
Peterson, Virginia. 2001. **Homeless: Struggling to Survive**. New York: Gale
Group. A discussion about why people are homeless, how the government
provides assistance to the homeless, and imparts information on hunger,
housing, and health issues.
Rebman, Renee C. 2001. **Runaway Teens: A Hot Issue**. Hot Issues series. Berkeley Heights, NJ: Enslow. Explains why teens run away and how they become throwaways, what life on the streets is like, and explains why teen
runways are a national epidemic. Includes a further reading section, Web
addresses for helpful organizations, hotlines, and detailed chapter notes.

Organizations and Online Resources about Homelessness and Runaways

Legal Services Homelessness Task Force
National Housing Law Project
122 C Street NW
Suite 740
Washington, DC 20001
(202) 783-5140
   Uses legal means to advocate for the homeless at local, state, and federal lev-
els.

National Alliance to End Homelessness, Inc.
1518 K Street NW
Suite 206

Washington, DC 20005
(202) 638-1526
naeh@naeh.org
http://www.endhomelessness.org
   This group's goal is to end homelessness by changing federal policy and helping local members serve more homeless people.

National Center for Missing and Exploited Children
http://www.missingkids.org

National Runaway Hotline
(800) 621-4000

National Runaway Switchboard
http://www.nrscrisisline.org

Vanished Children's Alliance
991 W. Hedding Street, Suite 101
San Jose, CA 95126
1-800-VANISHED
(408) 296-1113
bhammond@vca.org
http://www.vca.org

Youth Crisis Hotline
(800) 448-4663
1800hithome@horizonsd.org
http://www.1800hithome.com/home/

Videos about Homelessness

No Home of Your Own: A Look into the Lives of Homeless Youth. 2004. 18 minutes. Video. New York: Educational Video Center. Learn about the issues
   faced by homeless youth living in New York City. Find out how teens become homeless, how homelessness has an impact on education, and what
   services are available for homeless youth.

Nonfiction about Homeschooling

Adams-Gordon, Beverly. 2000. **Home School, High School, and Beyond: A Time
   Management, Career Exploration, Organization, and Study Skills
   Course**. New York: Castlemoyle Books. Filled with a great deal of infor-
   mation for teens on homeschooling.

Barfield, Rhonda. 2002. **Real-Life Homeschooling: The Stories of 21 Families Who Teach Their Children at Home**. New York: Fireside Books. The author, who homeschools her four children, presents stories about families who also have decided to homeschool. The families are diverse, including those who live in the city, in rural areas, and are of various religious backgrounds. The families all face different types of challenges in homeschooling. For example, one family homeschools their children while at the same raising a child with Down Syndrome. Each story includes the names and ages of the family members and the best and worst advice that homeschooling parents have for others who are planning to pursue homeschooling.

Cohen, Cafi. 2000. **And What about College? How Homeschooling Leads to Admission to the Best Colleges and Universities**. New York: Holt Associates. Provides advice to homeschooled teens about being admitted to colleges and universities throughout the country.

Fiction about ESL and Immigrant Teens

Bartoletti, Susan Campbell. 2000. **A Coal Miner's Bride: The Diary of Anetka Kaminska**. Dear America series. New York: Scholastic. A diary account of thirteen-year-old Anetka, who immigrated to Lattimer, Pennsylvania, from Poland, married a coal miner, became a widow, and finally found her true love.

Chambers, Veronica. 2001. **Quinceañera Means Sweet 15**. New York: Hyperion. Eagerly anticipating her Quinceañera, the fifteenth birthday celebration that will signify her adulthood, Marisol is troubled by a lack of money, her mother's new boyfriend, changes in her best friend, and the absence of the father she never knew.

Gallo, Donald R., ed. 2004. **First Crossing: Stories about Teen Immigrants**. New York: Candlewick Press. Stories of recent Mexican, Venezuelan, Kazakh, Chinese, Romanian, Palestinian, Swedish, Korean, Haitian, and Cambodian immigrants reveal what it is like to face prejudice, language barriers, and homesickness.

Mead, Alice. 2005. **Swimming to America**. New York: Farrar, Straus and Giroux. Linda Berati, an eighth grader in Brooklyn, whose parents are Albanian, finds that her friend Ramon, a Cuban immigrant, is able to understand the confusion associated with her identity.

Mendoza, Louis, and S. Shankar, eds. 2003. **Crossing into America: The New Literature of Immigration**. New York: The New Press. Features stories, poems, cartoons, newspaper stories, and memoirs of writers born in Mexico, Cuba, Kashmir, the Philippines, South Africa, Romania, and elsewhere. Although the book was published for adult readers, it will appeal to teens

who are interested in reading about how immigrants have succeeded in
the United States.

Na, An. 2001. **A Step from Heaven**. Asheville, NC: Front Street. Winner of the
Michael L. Printz Award, this book details the experiences of a Korean girl
who finds it difficult to learn English and adjust to life in America.

Osa, Nancy. 2003. **Cuba 15**. New York: Delacorte. Violet Paz, a Chicago high
school student, reluctantly prepares for her upcoming "quince," a Spanish
nickname for the celebration of a Hispanic girl's fifteenth birthday.

Ryan, Pam Muñoz. 2000. **Esperanza Rising**. New York: Scholastic. Esperanza and
her mother are forced to leave their life of wealth and privilege in Mexico
to work in the labor camps of Southern California, where they must adapt
to the harsh circumstances facing Mexican farm workers on the eve of the
Great Depression.

Stine, Catherine. 2003. **Refugees**. New York: Delacorte. Following the September
11, 2001 terrorist attacks, Dawn, a sixteen-year-old runaway from San Francisco, connects by phone and e-mail with Johar, a gentle fifteen-year-old
Afghani who assists Dawn's foster mother, a doctor, at a Red Cross refugee
camp in Peshawar.

Veciana-Suarez, Ana. 2002. **Flight to Freedom**. New York: Scholastic. Writing in
the diary that her father gave her, thirteen-year-old Yara describes life with
her family in Havana, Cuba, in 1967.

Nonfiction about ESL and Immigrant Teens

Boguchwal, Sherry. 2000. **ESL Beginner**. Piscataway, NJ: Research and Education
Association. Designed for people taking ESL and adult education classes,
this book provides exercises on nouns, verbs, simple sentences, compound
sentences, grammar, reading, and listening. The first chapter explains how
the book is organized, gives advice to the instructor, and includes a student progress sheet.

Currie, Stephen. 2000. **Issues in Immigration**. San Diego, CA: Lucent Books.
This book discusses the following issues: whether assimilation should
be a priority for immigrants, does immigration harm U.S. workers,
should immigrants be denied governmental services, should efforts to
halt illegal immigration be strengthened, and if immigration policies
should be reformed. Includes a list of organizations to contact for more
information.

Hay, Jeff, ed. 2001. **Immigration**. San Diego, CA: Greenhaven Press. This collection of essays explores the history of immigration, with two chapters devoted to immigration from Asia and Mexico.

Santos, Edward J. 2002. **Everything You Need to Know If You and Your Parents
Are New Americans**. Need to Know Library series. New York: Rosen. Es-

pecially useful for reluctant readers and for teens learning English as a second language, this book includes a glossary, photographs, and statistics about becoming an American. After explaining the history of immigration in the United States, there is information about getting into the country and how to keep in touch with one's original culture.

Organizations and Online Resources about ESL and Immigrant Teens

Advocates for Language Learning
PO Box 4952
Culver City, CA 90231
(301) 313-3333

American Immigration Center
(800) 814-1555
http://www.us-immigration.com

Association of MultiEthnic Americans
PO Box 66061
Tucson, AZ 85728
(877) 954-2632
http://www.ameasite.org

Immigration History Research Center
University of Minnesota
College of Liberal Arts
311 Andersen Library
222 21st Avenue S
Minneapolis, MN 55455
(612) 625-4800
http://www.umn.edu/ihrc

National Latino Children's Institute
321 El Paso Street
San Antonio, TX 78207
(210) 228-9997
http://www.nlci.org
http://www.Foreignborn.com
    Geared for those who are foreign born and living or entering the United States.

United States Immigration and Naturalization Service (INS)
http://www.ins.usdoj.gov/graphics/index.html
   Statistics, laws, information, and forms about naturalization and immigration.

Fiction about Pregnant and Parenting Teens

Baur, Tricia. 2000. **Shelterbelt**. New York: St. Martin's Press. After deciding that
   she cannot tell her father and his pro-life girlfriend that she wants an abortion, Jade, a pregnant teenager in Paradise, Nebraska, drops out of school,
   becomes a nanny, and has her baby.
Bechard, Margaret. 2002. **Hanging on to Max**. Brookfield, CT: Roaring Brook
   Press. When his girlfriend decides to give their baby away, Sam, age seventeen, is determined to keep him and raise him alone.
Bennett, James W. 2001. **Plunking Reggie Jackson**. New York: Simon and Schuster. High school baseball star Coley Burke tries to deal with an ankle in-
   jury, back spasms, a pregnant girlfriend, academic failure, pressure from
   his father, and the legacy of his dead older brother.
———. 2003. **Faith Wish**. New York: Holiday House. Upset with the course her
   life has taken, popular senior Anne-Marie is drawn to Brother Jackson, the
   leader of a cultlike Christian group, becomes pregnant by him, and runs
   away to figure out what the Lord wants her to do.
Brinkerhoff, Shirley. 2000. **Second Choices**. Minneapolis, MN: Bethany House.
   Nikki struggles with a relationship that may be leading her away from
   God, giving up her baby for adoption, and explaining her feelings about
   abortion to her classmates amidst dangerous vandalism at school.
Bunting, Eve. 2000. **Doll Baby**. New York: Houghton Mifflin. A fifteen-year-old
   girl who is pregnant decides she wants to keep her baby.
Feinberg, Anna. 2000. **Borrowed Light**. New York: Delacorte. A sixteen-year-old
   feels alienated from her family as she struggles with the difficult decisions
   surrounding her unplanned pregnancy.
Halpern, Sue. 2003. **The Book of Hard Things: A Novel**. New York: Farrar, Straus
   and Giroux. Cuzzy Gage, age eighteen, has always lived in poverty in the
   isolated mountain hamlet where he was born. His girlfriend, the mother
   of his child, is determined that he will remain there.
Horniman, Joanne. 2003. **Mahalia**. New York. Alfred A. Knopf. This book chronicles a teen father's struggle to be a good parent.
Hrdlitschka, Shelley. 2002. **Dancing Naked**. New York: Orca Books. Kia, age sixteen and pregnant, learns how to confront her own fears and those of her
   parents and her friends from her church and youth group.
Leavitt, Caroline. 2004. **Girls in Trouble**. New York: St. Martin's Press. Abandoned by her boyfriend and at odds with her parents for choosing open
   adoption, Sara, a sixteen-year-old honor student, is sustained by her relationship with her daughter's adoptive parents until they become threat-

ened by her increasing obsession with the baby and make a decision that has devastating consequences for everyone.

McDonald, Janet. 2002. **Chill Wind**. New York: Farrar, Straus and Giroux. Afraid that she will have nowhere to go when her welfare checks have stopped, high school dropout Aisha, age nineteen, tries to figure out how she can support herself and her two young children in New York City.

Oughton, Jerrie. 2003. **Perfect Family**. Boston: Houghton Mifflin. When Welcome, a fifteen-year-old girl living in a small town in North Carolina during the 1950s, finds out that she is pregnant, she faces some important decisions.

Pennebaker, Ruth. 2001. **Don't Think Twice**. New York: Henry Holt. Seventeen-year-old and pregnant, Anne lives with other unwed mothers in a group home in rural Texas where she learns to be herself before giving her child up for adoption.

Picoult, Jodi. 2000. **Plain Truth**. New York: Pocket Books. In the small town of Paradise, Pennsylvania, Katie Fisher, age eighteen and an unwed Amish woman, gives birth to a live baby in a barn, but suspicions arise when the baby is found dead.

Plummer, Louise. 2001. **A Dance for Three**. New York: Laurel Leaf. When fifteen-year-old Hannah becomes pregnant and her rich, popular boyfriend claims he is not responsible, she is forced to face some hard facts about her life.

Porter, Connie. 2000. **Imani All Mine**. Boston: Houghton Mifflin. Tasha is fifteen and the mother of a baby in the inner city.

Wild, Margaret. 2004. **One Night**. New York: Random House. In this novel written in free verse and narrated by alternating characters, a teenaged girl decides to have her baby and care for it on her own after a "one night stand" results in pregnancy.

Winston, Sherri. 2004. **Acting: A Novel**. New York: Marshall Cavendish. Longing to escape from her small Michigan town, sixteen-year-old Eve, an aspiring actress, is forced to confront both her family's and her own expectations when her twin sister announces her pregnancy.

Zeises, Lara M. 2004. **Contents under Pressure**. New York: Delacorte. Lucy, a fourteen-year-old high school freshman, experiences the happiness and confusion of dating a popular older boy, changing relationships with life-long friends, and sharing a bedroom with her older brother's pregnant girl-friend.

Nonfiction about Pregnant and Parenting Teens

Cothran, Helen, ed. 2001. **Teen Pregnancy and Parenting**. <u>Current Controversies</u> series. San Diego, CA: Greenhaven. Includes essays by several authors including topics such as whether teenage pregnancy is a serious problem, what factors contribute to teenage pregnancy, how teenage pregnancy can be prevented, alternatives that exist for pregnant teens, and whether society should approve of teenage parenting. There is an extensive bibliography appropriate for teenagers and a list of organizations to contact for further information.

Davis, Deborah. 2004. **You Look Too Young to Be a Mom: Teen Mothers Speak Out on Love, Learning, and Success**. New York: Penguin. Firsthand accounts from teen moms who have defied negative stereotypes, overcame challenges, and found paths to success.

Endersbe, Julie. 2000. **Teen Fathers: Getting Involved**. Mankato, MN: Life Matters. Discusses problems and dilemmas faced by teenage males when they become fathers and identifies options and solutions available for them.

Gottfried, Ted. 2001. **Teen Fathers Today**. Brookfield, CT: Twenty-First Century Books. Presents real-life stories about teen fathers and gives advice on dealing with the reactions of parents, the mother's pregnancy, and taking responsibility.

Haller, Tania. 2002. **Pregnant! What Can I Do? A Guide for Teenagers**. Jefferson, NC: McFarland. Provides information about options for pregnant teenagers, including abortion, adoption, and pregnancy.

Hurley, Jennifer A. 2001. **The Ethics of Abortion**. Opposing Viewpoints series. San Diego, CA: Greenhaven Press. Several essays explore the social, moral, medical, and political aspects concerning abortion.

Lindsay, Jeanne Warren. 1999. **Nurturing Your Newborn: Young Parent's Guide to Baby's First Month**. Buena Park, CA: Morning Glory Press. Gives information for teenage mothers about caring for their infants and themselves.

————. Illustrated by Jami Moffett. 2000. **Do I Have a Daddy? A Story about a Single-Parent Child with a Special Section for Single Mothers and Fathers**. Buena Park, CA: Morning Glory Press. This is a children's book that may be appropriate for teen parents to utilize with their children. In the book, a single mother explains to her son that his daddy left soon after he was born. Includes a section with suggestions for answering the question, "Do I have a daddy?"

McDowell, Josh. 2000. **My Friend Is Struggling With—Unplanned Pregnancy**. Project 911 Collection series. Nashville, TN: World Publishers. Uses the story of a pregnant high school senior to deal with issues related to teen pregnancy from a Christian perspective.

Natterson, Cara Familian. 2004. **Your Newborn: Head to Toe; Everything you want to Know about Your Baby's Health through the First Year**. New York: Little, Brown. Natterson, a pediatrician, provides practical medical advice about the first year of life, including information about the hospital experience, Apgar scores, and problems that may arise. Although not specifically written for teenagers, this book will be useful to new mothers of any age.

Nelson, Kevin. 2004. **The Everything Father-to-Be Book: A Survival Guide for Men**. Avon, MA: Adams Media. Provides practical advice to future fathers including information about time and money pressures, supporting the mother and child, diapers, formula, and more.

Pollock, Sudie. 2001. **Will the Dollars Stretch? Teen Parents: Living on Their Own; Virtual Reality through Stories and Check-writing Practice**. Buena Park, CA: Morning Glory Press. Stories of teen parents accompanied by exercises providing practice for the reader in writing checks and in meeting the real challenges of living within a tight budget.

South Vista Educational Center. 2000. **Daycare and Diplomas: Teen Mothers Who Stay in School**. Minneapolis, MN: Fairview Press. Eighteen young mothers describe what it is like to juggle schedules, family pressures, job responsibilities, and schoolwork while raising a child.

Board Games for Pregnant and Parenting Teens

Morning Glory Press
6595 San Haroldo Way
Buena Park, CA 90620
(888) 327-4362
http://www.morningglorypress.com

Baby's First Year

Challenge of Toddlers

Pregnancy and Newborn Journey

Two-in-One Pregnancy Bingo

Organizations and Online Resources for Pregnant and Parenting Teens

Adolescent Wellness and Reproductive (AWARE) Foundation
1015 Chestnut Street, Suite 1225
Philadelphia, PA 19107-4302
(215) 955-9847
(215) 923-3474
http://www.awarefoundation.org

The mission of this foundation is to educate adolescents about making responsible decisions about wellness, sexuality, and reproductive health.

Advocates for Youth
1025 Vermont Avenue NW, Suite 200
Washington, DC 20005
(202) 347-5700
Info@advocatesforyouth.org
http://www.advocatesforyouth.org
   Provides information, education, and advocacy to youth-serving agencies, policy makers, and the media about pregnancy and HIV prevention among young people.

American Coalition for Fathers and Children
22365 El Toro Road
No. 335
Lake Forest, CA 92630
(800) 978-DADS

American Pregnancy Association
1425 Greenway Drive, Suite 440
Irving, Texas 75038
(800) 672-2296
   This national organization promotes reproductive wellness through research, advocacy, education, and community awareness.

Fatherhood Project
http://www.fatherhoodproject.org
   Education project supporting men's involvement in child rearing.

Healthy Teen Network (formerly the National Organization on Adolescent Pregnancy, Parenting, and Prevention)
509 Second Street NE
Suite 200
Washington, DC 20002
(202) 547-8814
(202) 547-8815
healthyteens@healthyteennetwork.org
   The mission of this group is to provide resources, information, education, and leadership related to healthy teens, specifically pregnant teens.

Institute for Responsible Fatherhood and Family Revitalization
9500 Arena Drive
Suite 400
Largo, MD 20774
(301) 773-2044
CharlesBallard@responsiblefatherhood.org

Helps reunite fathers with their children and provides family outreach support and counseling.

La Leche League
1400 North Meacham Road
Schaumburg, IL 60173
(947) 519-7730
http://www.lalecheleague.org
This organization provides support to mothers who are breastfeeding. The Web site provides specific information about how La Leche League leaders can help parenting teens feel more comfortable about breastfeeding. They emphasize the advantages of breastfeeding and help to make teen mothers feel comfortable at La Leche League meetings.

MELD for Young Dads
123 North 3rd Street
Suite 507
Minneapolis, MN 55401
Provides education and support for teen fathers. Offers career help, stress relief, and health and development classes.

Medline Plus
http://www.medlineplus.gov

U.S. National Library of Medicine
8600 Rockville Pike
Bethesda, MD 20894
Includes information on 650 different health topics including a section for pregnant teens that provides links to further information.

National Campaign to Prevent Teen Pregnancy
1776 Massachusetts Avenue NW
Suite 200
Washington, DC 20036
(202) 478-8500
campaign@teenpregnancy.org
http://www.teenpregnancy.org
The goal of this organization is to reduce teen pregnancy.

National Fatherhood Initiative
http://www.fatherhood.org
Current information on increasing involvement of fathers in the lives of their children.

National Institute for Responsible Fatherhood
8555 Hough Avenue
Cleveland, OH 44106
(216) 791-1468

National Youth Crisis Hotline
(800) 448-4663

Girl-Mom
http://www.girlmom.com
   A site dedicated to empowering and fighting the stereotypes about teenage
mothers.

Fiction about Sexuality

Brashares, Ann. 2001. **The Sisterhood of the Traveling Pants**. New York: Delacorte. Four best friends experience magic through an ordinary pair of
   pants.
———. 2003. **The Second Summer of the Sisterhood.** New York: Delacorte. This
   work is the sequel to **The Sisterhood of the Traveling Pants**, in which Bridget, Lena, Carmen, and Tiby embark on their sixteenth summer.
Brian, Kate. 2004. **The V Club**. New York: Simon and Schuster. Four high school
   friends pledge to maintain their virginity in order to exemplify the purity
   required to win a scholarship.
Burgess, Melvin. 2004. **Doing It**. New York: Henry Holt. Three teenage friends,
   Dino, Jonathon, and Ben, confront the confusions, fears, and joys of adolescent male sexuality.
Cann, Kate. 2001. **Sex**. New York: HarperCollins. Having finally given in and had
   sex with her boyfriend, sixteen-year-old Coll finds that the decision has
   drastically changed their relationship. Other books in this trilogy include
   Ready? (HarperCollins, 2001) and **Go!** (HarperCollins, 2001).
Carlson, Melody. 2004. **Torch Red: Color Me Torn**. Colorado Springs, CO: Think
   Books. Feeling like she is the only virgin on the planet, a high school junior wrestles with questions about love and sex before ultimately choosing
   to give herself to God instead of her boyfriend. Other books in the series
   include **Dark Blue: Color Me Lonely** (NavPress, 2004) and **Deep Green:
   Color Me Jealous** (NavPress, 2004).
Cart, Michael. 2001. **Love and Sex: Ten Stories of Truth**. New York: Simon and
   Schuster. A collection of short stories about sex and love by popular au-
   thors including Laurie Halse Anderson, Angela Johnson, Chris Lynch,
   Garth Nix, and more.
Perez, Marlene. 2004. **Unexpected Development**. Brookfield, CT: Roaring Brook
   Press. In a series of papers for her Honors English class, a senior in high-

school relates the difficulties of being blessed with a voluptuous body that began to develop in fifth grade.

Zeises, Lara M. 2002. **Bringing Up the Bones**. New York: Delacorte. Bridget Edelstein mourns the loss of her high school boyfriend who died in a car crash and rebounds with a new love after engaging in a one-night stand.

Nonfiction about Sexuality

Bailey, Jacqui. 2004. **Sex, Puberty, and All That Stuff: A Guide to Growing Up**. New York: Barron's. Discusses hormones, sex, dating, and birth control.

Basso, Michael J. 2003. **The Underground Guide to Teenage Sexuality**. Minneapolis, MN: Fairview Press. Presents facts about human sexuality, including anatomy, sexually transmitted diseases, contraception, homosexuality, and sexual intercourse.

Clausener-Petit, Magali. 2004. **Sex Explained: Honest Answers to Your Questions about Guys and Girls, Your Changing Body, and What Really Happens during Sex**. New York: Amulet Books. Answers questions about the male and female body, sex, orgasms, masturbation, and sexually transmitted diseases.

Hatchell, Deborah. 2003. **What Smart Teenagers Know . . . about Dating, Relationships and Sex**. Santa Barbara, CA: Piper Books. Explores all aspects of relationships including flirting, dating, sex, meeting parents, and breaking up.

Herman, Doug. 2004. **Come Clean: It's a Pure Revolution; It's about Sex, It's about Your Future, It's about What You Deserve**. Wheaton, IL: Tyndale House. This work discusses the benefits of remaining abstinent from a Christian perspective.

Lange, Donna. 2005. **Taking Responsibility: A Teen's Guide to Contraception and Pregnancy**. Broomall, PA: Mason Crest. Covers reproductive systems, abstinence, birth control, pregnancy, parenting, and adoption.

Lookadoo, Justin. 2004. **The Dirt on Sex: A Dateable Book**. Grand Rapids, MI: Hungry Planet. Discusses sex in relation to religion, ethics, abstinence, homosexuality, pregnancy, and more.

Shaw, Tucker. 2000. **This Book Is about Sex**. New York: Alloy Books. Provides information about sex, contraceptives, sexually transmitted diseases, masturbation, and more.

Organizations and Online Resources about Sexuality

National AIDS Hotline
(800) 342-2437

Planned Parenthood Federation of America
810 Seventh Avenue
New York, NY 10019
communications@ppfa.org
http://www.ppfa.org/ppa/
    A national organization that supports people's right to make their own repro-
ductive decisions without governmental interference.

SEX, Etc.
http://www.sxetc.org
    A Web site by teens for teens, provides a forum for teenagers to learn about is-
sues related to sexuality. Includes writings by teens, polls, message boards, and
links to information about love, abortion, adoption, GLBTQ issues, sexually transmitted diseases, and more.

Network for Family Life Education
Center for Applied Psychology
Rutgers University
41 Gordon Road
Suite A
Piscataway, NJ 08854
(732) 445-7929
(732) 445-7970 (fax)
sexetc@rci.rutgers.edu
http://www.sxetc.org/index.php

Sexuality Information and Education Council of the U.S. (SIECUS)
130 West 42nd Street
Suite 350
New York, NY 10036-7802
SIECUS@siecus.org
http://www.siecus.org

Fiction about Same-sex Parents and Gay, Lesbian, Bisexual, Transgender, and Questioning Teens

General

Summer, Jane, ed. 2004. **Not the Only One: Lesbian and Gay Fiction for Teens**.
    Los Angeles, CA: Alyson Publications. This anthology for gay and lesbian
    teens features fiction by authors including Brent Hartinger, Claire McNab,
    Michael Thomas Ford, and Bonnie Shimko.

Bisexuality

Ryan, Sara. 2001. **Empress of the World**. New York: Viking. While attending a sum-
    mer institute, fifteen-year-old Nic meets another girl named Battle, falls in
    love with her, and finds the relationship to be difficult and confusing.

Gays

De Oliveira, Eddie. 2004. **Lucky**. New York: Scholastic. Toby, age nineteen, reflects
    back on events during his first year of college when he explored his sex-
    ual identity.

Ferris, Jean. 2000. **Eight Seconds**. San Diego, CA: Harcourt. John, age eighteen,
    must confront his own sexuality when he goes to rodeo school and finds
    himself strangely attracted to an older boy who is smart, tough, compli-
    cated, gorgeous, and gay.

Freymann-Weyr, Garret. 2002. **My Heartbeat**. Boston, MA: Houghton Mifflin. As
    she tries to understand the closeness between her older brother and his
    best friend, fourteen-year-old Ellen finds her relationship with each of
    them changing.

Hartinger, Brent. 2003. **Geography Club: A Young Adult Novel**. New York:
    HarperCollins. Russel, a high school sophomore, and three other gay stu-
    dents set up a club for gay and lesbian students.

Koja, Kathe. 2005. **Talk**. New York: Farrar, Straus and Giroux. Kit is hiding a se-
    cret, but his best friend, Carma, has figured it out. When Kit participates
    in the high school play as the male lead, he focuses his attention on Pablo,
    another boy in school.

Levithan, David. 2003. **Boy Meets Boy**. New York: Alfred A. Knopf. Paul, a soph-
    omore, finds that he is attracted to another boy, Noah.

Malloy, Brian. 2002. **The Year of Ice**. New York: St. Martin's Press. Kevin, age sev-
    enteen, struggles with a crush on his best friend while also trying to main-
    tain a good relationship with his father after his mother is killed. This book
    won an Alex Award in 2003.

Mastbaum, Blair. 2004. **Clay's Way**. Los Angeles, CA: Alyson Books. Fifteen-year-
    old Sam, a wanna-be punk rocker, becomes obsessed with Clay, a
    seventeen-year-old surfer.

Quinn, Jay. 2001. **Metes and Bounds**. New York: Harrington Park Press. The sum-
    mer after graduating from high school, while living on the coast of North
    Carolina, Matt, age eighteen, reminisces about Chris, his former boyfriend,
    and engages in sexual encounters with new acquaintances.

Sanchez, Alex. 2001. **Rainbow Boys**. New York: Simon and Schuster. Three gay
    teens describe their life experiences during their senior year in high school.
———. 2003. **Rainbow High**. New York: Simon and Schuster. Follows three gay
    high school seniors as they struggle with issues of coming out, safe sex,
    homophobia, being in love, and college choices.

————. 2004. **So Hard to Say**. New York: Simon and Schuster. Thirteen-year-old Xio, a Mexican American girl, and Frederick, who has just moved to California from Wisconsin, quickly become close friends, but when Xio starts thinking of Frederick as her boyfriend, he must confront his feelings of confusion and face the fear that he might be gay.

Storandt, William. 2002. **The Summer They Came: A Novel**. New York: Villard Books. Anthony, age eighteen, a waiter in the seaside town of Long Spit in Rhode Island, comes to terms with his sexuality when his formerly sleepy town is transformed into a gay hot spot.

Taylor, William. 2003. **Pebble in a Pool**. Los Angeles, CA: Alyson Books. Paul, a high school senior, becomes more aware of his sexuality after his fundamentalist father kicks him out of the house and he begins living with a local artist.

Yates, Bart. 2004. **Leave Myself Behind**. New York: Kensington Books. In this Alex Award–winning book, Nick, age seventeen, falls in love with the boy next door.

Lesbians

Bechdel, Alison. 2003. **Dykes and Sundry Other Carbon-based Life Forms to Watch Out For**. Los Angeles, CA: Alyson Publications. This groundbreaking, nationally syndicated comic strip celebrates twenty years in print with a tenth collection that explores the lives of its characters in a post-millennium, post 9-11 America.

Benduhn, Tea. 2003. **Gravel Queen**. New York: Simon and Schuster. All Aurin wants to do the summer before her senior year in high school is hang out with her friends Kenny and Fred, but when she falls in love with Neila, everything changes.

Brown, Rita Mae. 2001. **Alma Mater**. New York: Ballantine Books. In this lesbian coming-of-age story, Victoria "Vic" Savadge, age twenty-two, discovers her fate at a small Virginia college.

Brownrigg, Sylvia. 2001. **Pages for You**. New York: Farrar, Straus and Giroux. Flannery, age seventeen, a student at an Ivy League school, falls in love with a teaching assistant who is eleven years older.

Johnson, Maureen. 2004. **The Bermudez Triangle**. New York: Razorbill. The friendship of three high school girls and their relationships with their friends and families are tested when two of them fall in love with each other.

Myracle, Lauren. 2003. **Kissing Kate**. New York: Dutton. Lissa feels alone after she and her best friend, Kate, share a kiss.

Peters, Julie Anne. 2005. **Far from Xanadu**. New York: Little, Brown. Mike's life is turned upside down when she meets Xanadu, a new student who is complicated and sexy.

Watts, Julia. 2001. **Finding H. F.** Los Angeles, CA: Alyson Books. H. F. begins a re-
    lationship with Wendy, and the two embark on an adventure in which they
    meet homeless gay teens who have formed their own families.

Same-sex Parents

Garden, Nancy. 2000. **Holly's Secret**. New York: Farrar, Straus and Giroux. When
    she starts middle school, Holly, age eleven, decides to become sophisticated
    and feminine, and changes her name to Yvette, and hides the fact that her
    two moms are lesbians.
Halpin, Brendan. 2004. **Donorboy: A novel**. New York: Villard Books. When
    fourteen-year-old Rosalind's two lesbian parents die in an accident, she is
    forced to live with her father, whom she has only known as a sperm donor.
Shepherd, Pamela. 2003. **Zach at Risk**. New York: Alice Street Editions. Zach finds
    that society has difficulty accepting the fact that he is being raised by two
    lesbians.
Sones, Sonya. 2004. **One of Those Hideous Books Where the Mother Dies**. New
    York: Simon and Schuster. Fifteen-year-old Ruby Milliken leaves her best
    friend, her boyfriend, her aunt, and her mother's grave in Boston and re-
    luctantly flies to Los Angeles to live with her father, a famous movie star
    who divorced her mother before Ruby was born and lives with a man.

Transgender

Peters, Julie Anne. 2004. **Luna: A Novel**. New York: Little, Brown. Fifteen-year-
    old Regan's life, which has always revolved around keeping her older
    brother Liam's transexuality a secret, changes when Liam decides to start
    the process of "transitioning" by first telling his family and friends that he
    is a girl who was born in a boy's body.

Nonfiction for Gay, Lesbian, Bisexual, Transgender, and Questioning Teens

General

Bullough, Vern L. 2002. **Before Stonewall: Activists for Gay and Lesbian Rights
    in Historical Context**. Binghamton, NY: Haworth Press. An introduction
    to the lives and contributions of key figures in the history of the American
    lesbian and gay movement.
Huegel, Kelly. 2003. **GLBTQ: The Survival Guide for Queer and Questioning
    Teens**. Minneapolis, MN: Free Spirit. Describes the challenges faced by gay,
    lesbian, bisexual, and transgendered teens, offers practical advice, real-life
    experiences, and accessible resources and support groups.

Mann, William J. 2004. **Gay Pride: A Celebration of All Things Gay and Lesbian**. New York: Citadel Press. From Alexander the Great to Elton John, this inspiring, joyous book triumphantly commemorates the many ways gays and lesbians have profoundly shaped the face of the world's politics, art, literature, music, theatre, cinema, sports, civil rights, and so on.

Marcovitz, Hal, and George Gallup. 2005. **Teens and Gay Issues**. *The Gallup Youth Survey: Major Issues and Trends*. Broomall, PA: Mason Crest Publishers. Provides statistical information, stories, and reports related to teens and gay issues.

Rutledge, Leigh W. 2003. **The Book of Gay Lists**. Los Angeles, CA: Alyson Books. A collection of lists related to homosexuality, such as "Noteworthy Gay Firsts," "Famous Gay or Bisexual Men Who Served in the U.S. Military," and "Gay Winners of the Pulitzer Prize."

Sonnie, Amy. 2000. **Revolutionary Voices**. Los Angeles, CA: Alyson Books. Celebrates queer youth culture through a collection of prose, poetry, artwork, letters, and diaries written by people of various races, classes, and religion.

Bisexuality

Atkins, Dawn, ed. 2002. **Bisexual Women in the Twenty-first Century**. New York: Haworth Press. A collection of essays that explores all aspects of bisexuality and women. In "Bisexual Female Adolescents: A Critical Analysis of Past Research, and Results from a National Survey," authors Stephen T. Russell and Hinda Seif conclude that there is a prevalence of both-sex romantic relationships among young women and that adolescent females tend not to report both-sex attraction in surveys such as the National Longitudinal Study of Adolescent Health.

Orndorff, Kata. 1999. **Bi Lives: Bisexual Women Tell Their Stories**. Tucson, AZ: See Sharp Press. In-depth interviews with women who are bisexual, including those who are married, in group marriages, mothers, and so on.

Gays

Read, Kirk. 2001. **How I Learned to Snap: A Small-Town Coming-Out and Coming-of-Age Story**. New York: Hill Street Press. This memoir focuses on Read's experience of coming out in the 1980s.

Rich, Jason. 2002. **Growing Up Gay in America: Advice for Teen Guys Questioning Their Sexuality and Growing Up Gay**. New York: Franklin Street Books. Specifically aimed at older gay teen males, this book explores the gay social scene; provides advice about relationships and sex; gives words of advice about cyberspace; and supplies a detailed list of gay-friendly organizations, help lines, colleges, churches, and so on.

Lesbians

Faderman, Lillian. 2001. **Surpassing the Love of Men: Romantic Friendship and Love Between Women from the Renaissance to the Present**. New York: Quill. History of love between women.

Rashid, Norrina, ed., and Jane Hoy. 2000. **Girl2Girl: The Lives and Loves of Young Lesbian and Bisexual Women**. London: Diva Books. A collection of poems, advice, autobiographical information, and jokes by young women ages fourteen through twenty-one who are trying to cope in a homophobic world.

Same-sex Parents

Garner, Abigail. 2004. **Families Like Mine: Children of Gay Parents Tell It Like It Is**. New York: HarperCollins. The founder of FamiliesLikeMine.com reports on interviews with youth who have same-sex parents (http://www.familieslikemine.com).

Gottlieb, Andrew B. 2003. **Sons Talk about Their Gay Fathers**. New York: Harrington Park Press. Reports on the author's research of sons who have gay fathers. Includes a reference section, an index, and an interview guide.

Snow, Judith E. 2004. **How It Feels to Have a Gay or Lesbian Parent: A Book by Kids for Kids of All Ages**. New York: Harrington Park Press. In their own words, children of different ages talk about how they learned of their gay or lesbian parent's sexual orientation and the effect it has had on them.

Transgender

Xavier, Jessica, Courtney Sharp, and Mary Boenke. 2001. **Our Trans Children**. Washington, DC: Parents, Families and Friends of Lesbians and Gays. Details information about transgendered teens.

DVDs and Videos about Same-sex Parents and GLBTQ Teens

Assault on Gay America. 2000. 60 minutes. Video. Boston, MA: WGBH Educational Foundation. Explores the case of Billy Jack Gaithers, murdered in 1999, and includes interviews with his family members and friends.

Being Gay: Coming Out in the 21st Century. 2003. 25 minutes. DVD and video. Princeton, NJ: Films for the Humanities and Sciences. After giving historical information about homosexuality, viewers are given information about coming out and finding support.

Lipstick. 2002. 10 minutes. Video. Brooklyn, NY: Scenarios USA. Urged by her girlfriend, Emily, a high school student, decides to come out to her friends.

Our Mom's a Dyke. 1995. 23 minutes. Video. New York: Filmakers Library. This documentary explores the feelings of three adolescent girls when their mother comes out as a lesbian.

Reaching Out to Lesbian, Gay, and Bisexual Youth. 1997. 21 minutes. Video. New York: Cinema Guild. Relates the experiences of teens when they reveal their sexuality to their parents and friends. Interviews mental health professionals and gives advice on handling homophobia.

Scout's Honor. 2001. 60 minutes. Video. Harriman. NY: New Day Films. Explores the Boy Scouts of America and their stance on homosexuality.

Organizations and Online Resources for GLBTQ Teens

Gay and Lesbian Alliance Against Defamation (GLAAD)
248 West 35th Street
8th Floor
New York, NY 10001
(212) 629-3322
http://www.glaad.org
   This group works to promote and ensure fair, accurate, and inclusive representation of GLBTQ people and events.

Gay, Lesbian and Straight Education Network (GLSEN)
90 Broad Street
2nd Floor
New York, NY 10004
(212) 727-0135
glsen@glsen.org
http://www.glsen.org
   This organization works to create safe schools for students and offers resources and information on their Web site, including instructions for beginning a gay-straight alliance in schools.

Lambda Legal Defense and Education Fund
120 Wall Street
Suite 1500
New York, NY 10005
(212) 809-8585
legalhelpdesk@lambdalegal.org

http://www.lambdalegal.org
This group works to protect the civil rights of all GLBTQ people.

National Gay and Lesbian Task Force (NGLTF)
1325 Masssachussetts Avenue NW
Suite 600
Washington, DC 20005
(202) 393-5177
http://www.ngltf.org
Provides legal assistance and referrals to doctors, counselors, and other professionals. Maintains a publications library, offers scholarships for journalism students, and works to fight prejudice against GLBTQ people at local, state, and national levels.

OutProud: The National Coalition for Gay, Lesbian, Bisexual, and Transgender Youth
369 Third Street
Suite B-362
San Rafael, CA 94901
info@outproud.org
http://www.outproud.org
The Web site provides a great deal of information including suggested print and electronic resources, discussion groups, community role models, statistics, and news.

Parents, Families and Friends of Lesbians and Gays (PFLAG)
1726 M Street NW
Suite 400
Washington, DC 20036
(202) 467-8180
info@pflag.org
http://www.pflag.org
With chapters throughout the United States, this organization provides information and support for GLBTQ people, their friends, and family members.

Sexual Minority Youth Assistance (SMYAL)
410 7th Street SE
Washington, DC 20003
(202) 546-5940
http://www.smyal.org
Works to enhance the self-esteem of sexual minority youth ages thirteen through twenty-one.

Gay and Lesbian National Hotline
(888) THE-GLNH
glnh@glnh.org
http://www.glnh.org

National Hotline for Gay, Lesbian, Bisexual, and Transgender Youth
(800) 347-TEEN
   Sponsored by the Indianapolis Youth Group, this free hotline is staffed by
counselors and provides crisis counseling, information about shelters, and referrals.

All About Sex
http://www.allaboutsex.org
   A discussion site on sexuality with sections for young and older teens.

Coalition for Positive Sexuality
http://www.positive.org/Home/index.html
   "You have the right to complete and honest sex education," is this site's motto.
For sexually active teens or for those who are thinking about having sex.

TransProud
http://www.transproud.org
   Stories, resources, FAQs, and news relating to transgendered teens.

Trevor Helpline
(800) 866-4-U-TREVOR
http://www.thetrevorproject.org
   Crisis hotline for GLBTQ youth; Web site includes information about support
groups and resources for GLBTQ teens as well as advice about helping someone
who is suicidal.

Young Gay America
http://www.younggayamerica.com
   Provides a multitude of information about various topics related to teens and
includes interviews with GLBTQ teens throughout the country.

Youth.org
http://www.youth.org
   Includes links for GLBTQ teens, information, and a moderated bulletin board.

CONCLUSION

In 2004, I attended my fifteen-year high school reunion where I was surrounded by others who had survived parachute pants, the Reagan era, and Milli Vanilli. Looking back, I compared the information-seeking behavior and fiction interests of teens who graduated from high school in 1989 with today's teens. Without technological advances, we relied on books and, dreadfully, microfilm and microfiche for our informational needs in the 1980s. Although we had young adult fiction way back then, we did not have as many ways to find it. Now teens have access to lots of information, but do they know how to find it?

As a librarian, it is your duty to prepare current teens for their fifteen-year high school reunion! In the year 2020, will those thirtysomethings be thinking back to the days when they had to use the Internet to link to organizations instead of, say, just tapping into the computer chip that has been implanted in their brains? Will teens reflect on how their local public library helped them to succeed as an extreme teen by having a thorough, unbiased collection of materials?

WORKS CITED

Edwards, Margaret. 1969. **The Fair Garden and the Swarm of Beasts: The Library and the Young Adult**. New York: Hawthorn Books.

Garden, Nancy. 1982. **Annie on My Mind**. New York: Farrar, Straus and Giroux.

Head, Ann. 1967. **Mr. and Mrs. Bo Jo Jones**. New York: Putnam.

Hinton, S. E. 1967. **The Outsiders**. New York: Dell.

Salinger, J. D. 1951. **The Catcher in the Rye**. New York: Bantam.

FOR FURTHER READING

Carter, Betty. 2000. **Best Books for Young Adults**. Chicago: American Library Association.

Donelson, Kenneth L., and Alleen Pace Nilsen. 2005. **Literature for Today's Young Adults**. 7th ed. Boston, MA: Pearson.

Gillespie, John T., and Catherine Barr. 2003. **Best Books for High School Readers: Grades 9–12**. Englewood, CO: Libraries Unlimited.

———. 2004. **Best Books for Middle School and Junior High Readers: Grades 6–9**. Englewood, CO: Libraries Unlimited.

Herald, Diana Tixier. 2003. **Teen Genreflecting: A Guide to Reading Interests**. 2nd ed. Englewood, CO: Libraries Unlimited.

Jones, Patrick, Patricia Taylor, and Kirsten Edwards. 2003. **A Core Collection for Young Adults**. Teens@the library series. New York: Neal-Schuman.

MacGregor, Amanda M. 2004. "Let's (Not) Get It On: Girls and Sex in Young Adult Literature." *Voice of Youth Advocates* (February 26): 464–468.

O'Dell, Katie. 2002. **Library Materials and Services for Teen Girls**. Englewood, CO: Libraries Unlimited.

Sullivan, Ed. 2004. "Going All the Way: First-Time Sexual Experiences of Teens in Fiction." *Voice of Youth Advocates* 26 (February): 461–463.

4

BEYOND THE REGULAR ROUTINE: PROMOTING THE LIBRARY AND RESOURCES

Call it underground. Just don't call it advertising. Not if you're trying to sell your product to teens. Edgy efforts to connect with teen consumers have become common among apparel marketers such as Levi Strauss & Co. and VF Corp.'s Lee Dungarees. But similar tactics have begun to invade even the more traditional world of package-goods marketing.
—Stephanie Thompson, "Targeting Teens Means Building Buzz" **Advertising Age** 71, no. 13 (2000): 26

Let us invade the traditional world of marketing by packaging the library, its services, collections, and staff as a product that all teens, regardless of extremeness, want to open and experience! Teens do not have a lot of extra time, and librarians are competing with them for precious moments. You need to be on the cutting edge in your approach to promoting library services to a population that is typically difficult to reach. Like all teens, extreme teens also experience the three stages of adolescence and have similar, but slightly different, needs from the library.

PROMOTION ASSESSMENT

Before you plan your next big promotional push to teens, it is important to assess what the library already does to promote its services with this population. Are you reaching teens who are in high school by placing advertisements in school newspapers or in high school yearbooks? Are you connecting with schools and giving educators information about services and collections? Is there a similar effort to reach teens who are not in school? Does your library Web site have a section for teens? Does it contain information of interest to extreme teens? What about the library newsletter? Any print or electronic promotions your library does for teens should include diverse images of teens, including images of extreme teens.

Reach out to the community and let them know what the library already has to offer teens. Contact agencies and organizations such as those mentioned previously in this book and let them know that your library has services and information available to all teens. Distribute library newsletters or program flyers at these organizations.

Also, look internally and determine if you are promoting the library within the walls of your building. With a fresh eye, look around your library as if you are seeing it for the first time. If you were a teen, or an extreme teen, would you feel comfortable in the building? Would you wonder if the staff members represent diverse viewpoints? If not, perhaps the makeup of the staff should better reflect the community, just like the library collection should reflect the community's makeup. Are there smiling staff members and flyers about upcoming programs? You can purchase posters from the American Library Association that announce the latest award-winning books selected by YALSA members and other teens. Consider working with the library's public relations department to make sure that diversity is represented in library publications and through public service announcements. If there are many Spanish-speaking members in your community, have you asked local radio stations to give public service announcements in Spanish?

If you are not already providing these basic services to teens, it is important to begin doing so. It is difficult to promote the library to teens if you do not understand them in the first place. Like a retailer, it is necessary to know your market before you attempt to persuade buyers that they should buy your product. Knowledge and comprehension of adolescent psychology is vital to understanding the needs of teens, especially extreme teens. Use library databases to learn about modern teens. Do a simple search through the EBSCO masterfile or another database to learn about what today's teens are thinking, their buying habits, and what they dream about for the future.

Promoting Programs

Remember that you will need to promote library programs as a worthwhile service to teens who are already busy with many other commitments. The best way to do this is to think about the ways in which you can promote the library within your own community. Do you live in an area where a lot of people, including teens, commute to work and school, so that they are likely to listen to certain radio stations? If so, you might want to consider placing public service announcements with these stations. Also, many local radio stations have broadcasts that feature local citizens. You might want to set up an interview so that you can promote the library and its services. You would be amazed by how many people listen to local broadcasts. I was interviewed about the building plans for the Dover Public Library after our facilities' consultants released a study stating that the library is "woefully inadequate." People came out of the woodwork to let me know that they had heard the broadcast. One result of local interviews might be higher circulation statistics and door counts that could directly relate to publicity. I have found that whenever the library is featured in the media, there is an increase of usage at the library.

Local cable stations typically look for community members to feature on their shows, and this is another opportunity to promote library programs for extreme teens. Once you have had successful programs in the library, you might want to include a few extreme teens on a cable show. Of course, minors will probably require specific permission from parents and legal guardians. The Allen County Public Library in Fort Wayne, Indiana, houses the local public broadcasting television station right in the library, and this was an incredible help with promoting the library. Their Teen Advisory Group created the public service announcement for the summer reading program, filmed it in the Young Adults' Services Department, and the program's statistics soared. Although extreme teens were not the only group targeted for the summer reading program, you can adapt publicity to suit your needs. Including teens in the promotion is a plus because teens will be more likely to listen to other teens.

Remind your library administrators that you are willing to be in the limelight regarding services and programs. Often, library directors are interviewed for the newspaper, radio station, or local television station, especially if the library is undergoing some type of massive physical change or if there is a concern, such as a censorship issue. If youth service librarians are featured in the media more often, the public is more likely to view the library as a positive place for teens and children, despite outside concerns related to censorship, or, for instance, safety and security.

Also, consider local publications outside the mainstream for publicity. In Dover, the Teen Services Librarian subscribes to the Dover High School newspaper, where, on the back page of every issue, there is an advertisement about our reference services. In future years, we will prepare a half-page advertisement in the high school yearbook about the library. This will promote the library for years to come, and it may even influence the actions of these students once they are adults and have their own children and teenagers. A permanent reminder about the library in a high school yearbook is timeless. Another way to promote the library and its programs and services is to find out who produces local area maps. In Dover, the library is featured on maps that are given to visitors and real estate agents. In that way, newcomers will know where the library is located.

Convince your supervisor that you need to get out of the building more often—and off the public service desk—in order to become more aware of what is going on in the community. Find out where extreme teens are hanging out. Is it the local coffee shop? Is there a popular bookstore? Are pregnant and parenting teens gathering in Babies "R" Us on a regular basis? Do dual-enrollment students tend to spend time in a certain place during the short amount of time that they have between high school and college classes? Are high school dropouts hanging out at the local arcade? If you do not know, you might want to ask the local military recruiters in town. They typically scout young men and women who might be right for the service. The only way to find out the answers to these questions is to get outside the walls of your building and investigate.

A SENSE OF PLACE

The next time you walk into a retail store, notice your surroundings. Are you greeted with lots of light, wonderful smells, and useful signage? Or are you in the dark where it is dusty, dirty, and dingy, wondering where to go? Some librarians enjoy visiting other libraries when they travel. If you have done this, you have surely noticed that all libraries are not alike. Your first impression on entering the building may be that the staff needs customer service training, that the carpet needs to be replaced, and that there are few teenagers using the facility.

Extreme Teen Tidbits: Places to Promote Programs with Flyers

- The back of bathroom doors in the library, in schools, and places where teens hang out. Think about the last time you visited a nightclub; was there some type of publicity in this location? Or, perhaps a message from MADD or the state department of motor vehicles about drinking and driving?

- Any place where a pregnant or parenting teen might go in order to seek information. As a young adult librarian I have visited abortion clinics, the offices of Planned Parenthood, Catholic Charities, doctors offices, and hospitals. Be prepared, however, to walk through a picket line. It is an experience that you will probably never forget.

- In your own backyard! Well, not quite, but in your library. If you have a teen area, great! slap flyers everywhere. If not, ask that a bulletin board be placed somewhere near the teen collection. No teen collection? Oh no! Teens must be hanging out somewhere in the library, so place the flyers where they will actually see and read them.

- On library staff! No, I am not suggesting that library staff be forced to walk around with flyers on their backs, but you might want to create flashy buttons saying "Ask me about..." (whatever you are trying to promote). At two of the libraries where I have worked, staff members were given T-shirts promoting the summer reading program and they were encouraged to wear them to work and when they conducted school visits.

- I love a parade! Not really, but that is how the song goes. Buy a copy of *The Library Cart Precision Drill Team Manual* by Linda D. McCracken and Lynne Zeiher (McFarland and Co., 2001) and start planning for the next big parade in your community. In Dover, we have plenty from which to choose, but the one that reaches the most people, the Old Dover Days parade—when everyone dresses up like people from the Colonial era—is the best bet. The parade route goes right past the front of the library, and last year Senator Joseph Biden (D-DE) marched past our window and waved. What better way to promote the library to local, state, and national politicians, as well as the entire community (and extreme teens), than hand out flyers at a parade?

- Colleges and universities serving dual-enrollment students and possibly homeschoolers may have a bulletin board that you can use to reach this segment of the extreme teen population.

- Visit local bookstores and organizations serving GLBTQ youth and even gay and lesbian bars and nightclubs. If you think that minors are not in these places, think again. You may be able to talk to the own-

ers, explain your mission, and place a flyer on the back of the bathroom door.

- Your library's Web site! You are not physically "hanging" a flyer there,
  but the point is the same—you are trying to reach a specific audience.
  High school dropouts may spend, for instance, a lot of time online.
  Also, consider allowing extreme teens to help you with the publicity
  on the Web site, and allow them to assist with original Web site content. For more information on this process, read "A Case for Making
  Original Content Part of Your YA Web Page" (*Young Adult Library Services* 3 [Winter 2005]: 32–34) by Paula Brehm-Heeger.

This is where preventive librarianship enters the picture. I was a life-
guard for nine years, and one of the first lessons that the American Red
Cross taught me was about precautionary lifeguarding. This concept involves preventing problems before they happen, such as making sure that
drain covers do not pop off—causing a tripping hazard—when the swimming pool is overfilled, and that chemicals and equipment are properly
stored away.

Consider the library where you work and think of how you can engage
in preventive librarianship in relation to teens. Has the head of the reference department ensured that a reference librarian who does not work
well with young people is not asked to cover the desk when teens are
more likely to visit? Are there directional signs in languages other than
English if there are speakers of other languages in your community?
Based on their body language, is it obvious that staff members accept
homeless people? Has the library director agreed to place an advertisement about the library in the local "street" newspaper that is produced
and run by the homeless? If not, consider making that suggestion! Do you
notice that librarians are taking the time to speak with teens who may be
out of the ordinary for some reason? These are only a few examples of
how preventive librarianship can be used with extreme teens. Before a
problem surfaces, attack it head on and come up with solutions so that
extreme teens will want to use your services.

You may also need to consider the physical location of your library
building and whether it is a barrier to extreme teens. If your library is located in a remote area with a lack of public transportation, or sidewalks,
to the facility, it may be difficult for patrons to get to the building. Imagine a teen parent attempting to push a stroller down a busy street without sidewalks to visit the public library for a book on child care. It is not

likely to happen. Where are teen materials kept? Is there a teen space in your library? Is it easy to find, and adequately and comfortably furnished for all teens? Do restrooms include baby changing stations, in both the women's room and in the men's room?

Staff members should remain nonjudgmental when assisting extreme teens. In a utopian situation, other library patrons would be nonjudgmental as well. Although librarians cannot control the actions of the public, a well-run library will include clear policies and procedures for handling problem patrons. Even if you have the best services possible for extreme teens in your library, it is important to ensure that other patrons respect the diverse needs of anyone using the library building.

LEARNING FROM EXTREME TEENS

Once you have created a welcoming atmosphere, realize that extreme teens can be an asset to the library and its staff. Extreme teens have a lot to teach librarians and other teens. First, consider working with your library administration to find out if extreme teens (or even adults who were extreme as teens) could be part of the library board. Some library boards already do include teenagers, such as Harford County, Maryland, described by Audra Caplan in "Making a Difference: Harford County Public Library's Teen Board Member" (*Young Adult Library Services* 1, no. 2 [Winter 2003]: 9). Teens have been represented on that library's board since 1994, and each year a high school junior is selected to serve during his or her senior year in high school.

Since staff diversity is vital, consider hiring extreme teens to work at your library. If this is not practical (e.g., if nobody under age eighteen can work in your building), consider beginning a volunteer program for teens and reaching out to nontraditional youth. Local agencies and organizations who work with extreme teens in some capacity may have suggestions about teens who may be interested in volunteering. Extreme teens may have lots of talents that they can offer to the public library. Like other teen volunteers, it is necessary to assess their skills before assigning tasks. Perhaps extreme teens could help you develop a Web page for teens. If one already exists in your library, you can ask them to share their knowledge about their own lives and they can possibly offer information about Web sites and organizations that can be added to an information and referral section on your teen Web site.

Extreme teens can help you to assess how well you are promoting the library. You might want to conduct formal or informal surveys. Decorate a can, write "Canned Thoughts" on it, and allow teens to drop little hints about how you are doing. You might want to ask different questions each month, such as, "What kind of books would you like to read that the library does not have?" or "What do you like about the layout of the building?" If you do not want to ask specific questions, you might get good feedback by leaving the can on display, allowing teens to freely voice their opinions.

Another way to learn about whether extreme teens find the library appealing is to walk through the facility with them. They can give you advice about how to better promote library materials. Allow them to help you with book displays about different topics, such as the top books chosen by ESL teens, or a gay pride display during gay pride month. At the Allen County Public Library in Fort Wayne, Indiana, one of my staff members created a display titled "Out of the Past" for gay pride month. The bulletin board display included a design in the shape of a closet. When the doors opened, they revealed famous gays and lesbians throughout history. A collection of nonfiction books about these men and women was available on a book cart located beneath the display.

Extreme teens in your library may also be interested in producing bookmarks and pathfinders that can be used by other teens. The pathfinders could guide teens to accurate and current information. If your library typically gives out bookmarks or flyers about the library to new patrons, perhaps these can be tailored to include diverse populations. You may also want to conduct writing or art contests that relate to extreme teens. These materials can be used to promote the library. A program for extreme teens on blogging, for instance, may lead to increased time spent at the library. Perhaps the teen who enjoys keeping a blog will come back to use the library's computers. Maybe a homeless teen will take the promotional materials that you have created.

NETWORKING IN THE EXTREME TEEN COMMUNITY

An experience of mine will help you understand networking and how news travels fast. Having heard many complaints in Dover, Delaware from staff and the public about the library, I was planning to meet with my boss to discuss the issues. I also planned to give him a list of compliments to balance out some of the complaints. The day before we were supposed to meet, I got my hair cut. I did this on my lunch break, and because I was in a rush, I ended up going to a different salon. Time was not on my side. At the new place, the stylist who cut my hair only cut one side of my head. When I pointed this out to her, she said no, that I was wrong. I clearly showed her that yes, indeed, she had forgotten one side. She realized her mistake and cut the other side. That afternoon, I told people my story, including a neighbor, another library staff member, and a city employee. It occurred to me that I was engaging in normal behavior by spreading bad news, but did I once tell these same people that I love my stylist at my regular salon? No! So why was I telling them about my bad experience? I decided to tell this story to my boss the next day in order to illustrate my point that he is more likely to hear about bad things rather than good experiences.

The next day, I began to tell my boss the story, but he interrupted and said, "I know, I know, she forgot to cut one side of your head." Drumroll, please. I shook my head, smiled, and said, "Now you should understand. Only the bad news gets around." Especially in a medium-size town where I live, bad news travels fast. I had only told three people the story the day before, but somehow, the word had already reached my supervisor.

How does this relate to extreme teens in the library? A good way to use the knowledge of extreme teens to promote the library is through positive networking in the teen community. They can help spread the word about the benefits of library use. Remember that good news travels slowly, though, and that bad news travels quickly. If an extreme teen has a negative experience at the library, it is likely that the extreme teens in your area will find out about it. In order to build a community of library users, make sure that you are not sending the wrong message through your body language, actions, or attitudes.

Imagine giving a group of homeschooled teens a tour of the library. They are likely to let their friends know about the tour if it was a positive experience, even if their friends are not homeschooled. Suppose that you promote the library at a health facility for expectant moms, and attract pregnant teens to the library. If they find the information useful, the pregnant teens are likely to let other people know about it. Perhaps issuing library cards to ESL and immigrant teens will result in entire families using the library, thereby opening up a whole new world to them.

Bad experiences, though, can cause worse effects. If good experiences result in happy patrons, it is likely that bad experiences can drive people away from using the library. To get back to the story about my bad haircut, I had never bothered to tell anyone where I normally got my good haircuts, but they all knew the exact location of the place where I will never return for a trim!

Reach out to state and national organizations and agencies who serve teens who are extreme due to their educational or living situation, or sexual identity. You may want to join these groups or spend time talking to their members. Also, talk to other librarians throughout the country who have promoted the library and its resources to extreme teens who may have words of wisdom for you.

Since some extreme teens may not be able to visit the library, consider alternative ways to promote library services and collections outside of your building. Public service announcements and library publicity have already been mentioned as ways to attract and represent extreme teens. Some teens, however, will not have access to these promotional materials. Incarcerated youth, for example, typically do not have access to local newspapers, television, and radio. Library promotion to this group will require networking with staff at the detention centers. Similarly, dual-enrollment students may not be aware that the library has an abundance of materials that may be useful when they research and write college-level papers. Again, it is necessary to determine the makeup of your audience and promote the library based on individual needs.

ADMINISTRATIVE SUPPORT

Perhaps your director is Happy, whistling while working to allocate funds for young adult services. Or maybe your director is Sleepy or Sneezy, and not paying attention to what is happening with teens at your library. Some directors are eternally Grumpy. (Anderson 2005, 3)

At the 2004 American Library Association annual conference in Orlando, Florida, I presented a program with seven other panelists titled "It's Not Fantasyland: Directors Speak about Young Adult Services." C. Allen Nichols, Audra Caplan, Michael Cart, Bette Ammon, Stephen Crowley, Monique le Conge, Susan Riley, and I became the seven dwarfs—and Snow White. All of us work, or have worked, as library directors in public libraries, and we are all advocates for teen library services. As library directors, the group is diverse, although we also have a lot in common. Some of the panelists were a little grumpy about having to pretend to be a dwarf. Others were happy. One had to be Snow White since she was the YALSA president at the time. Meanwhile, we all agreed that the wisest among us should be Doc.

The point I am trying to make is that the library director has the power to make or break services to teens, especially extreme teens. As the holder of the purse strings, the maker of the rules, and the director of time allocation, yes, sometimes it is good to be king. Oftentimes, library patrons are unhappy with the library's service because of policies and procedures, but they will be happy if policies and procedures are fair and consistently enforced among all patrons. Extreme teens often bear the brunt of library policies because their circumstances are different. It is difficult for library administrators to bend the rules even when they realize that the rules are not fair to all library patrons. A homeless teen who cannot produce a picture identification may have difficulty getting a library card. Or, a dual-enrollment student may suffer if circulation policies restrict the number of materials that are allowed to be borrowed in a certain call-number area. This student may desperately need all of the books for an upcoming assignment.

If you are a librarian who wants your library director to be more supportive of promoting library services to extreme teens, let him or her know what you have done to reach these teens. For example, if you have programs for pregnant teens, ask them to complete program evaluation forms. Since library directors push a lot of paper, make sure to highlight any sections that you want your library director to notice. If you have created a Webliography or a bookmark about resources that pertain to a specialized group, let your library director know why the resources were valuable to teenagers in the community. When library administrators get positive feedback, the more likely they are to shift budget lines, accommodate schedule changes, and consider promotion of staff who are sincerely passionate about promoting the library to unique groups.

DO NOT JUST TALK, BOOKTALK

Once you have gotten teens into the library, or you have made connections in the community so that you can promote services at other locations, such as juvenile detention centers, consider the art of booktalking. Booktalking is a great way to promote books to teens. Successful booktalkers see themselves as performers on a stage. The last thing that teens want is the monotony of listening to an adult talk about a book that sounds dull or old-fashioned. Booktalkers who have the attention of their audiences do not just talk about books. Instead, they jazz up presentations, using flair and enthusiasm to bring the books to life.

Booktalking may be especially useful with extreme teens. Reluctant readers may become excited about reading after a book is promoted in an enticing way. Booktalking puts a face on the library as a fun place where topics of all types can be explored, and this is particularly important for reluctant male teen readers who may be more interested in reading nonfiction than fiction. Incarcerated teens have more free time for reading, but they may be self-conscious about reading if peers or gang members are witnessing the activity. Immigrant teens might crave information and stories about their home countries, or they may want to learn more about American popular culture so that they can fit in. Teens who are exploring their sexual identity may be comforted to know that books exist that show various sexual identities in a positive way.

Learning to Booktalk

So how do you learn to booktalk instead of just talking about books? First, delve into published materials about the topic. Some books and articles written about different ways to booktalk are in a list below.

Second, learn by watching others. Watch colleagues who booktalk and ask them to watch and critique your performances. Perhaps you can work together to improve your booktalking skills. When I managed a young adult services department, I assigned staff to work together in groups of two. Each pair was responsible for utilizing different booktalking methods and for presenting their booktalks to the department at staff meetings. That way, staff could observe each others' techniques and offer ways in which they would present the booktalk differently.

Since booktalking is a performance, it is also beneficial to listen to recorded books and watch television and movies for ideas about interesting ways to portray information to an audience. Another way to learn about booktalking is to attend workshops on booktalking at library conferences. At the Indiana Library Federation (ILF) conference, Brad Howell of the Anderson, Indiana, Public Library and I presented a workshop for librarians on booktalking. Brad stayed out in the hallway while I introduced the presentation to the audience. In a tone as boring as possible, I told the audience my name and where I work. After that, I said, "Today we are going to tell you how to booktalk. Brad Howell is also a presenter, but he is in the bathroom at this time. So I will start without him. The first book I want to tell you about is called *Kissing Doorknobs* by Terry Spencer Hesser. This book is about a girl with a disease. I highly recommend this book. In the book, the main character has a problem controlling her actions."

At that very moment, Brad rushed into the room, out of breath, wiping his wet hands on his pants, and pranced around, saying, "Sheila! You won't believe what just happened in the bathroom! A guy did not wash his hands. In this day and age, how could someone not wash their hands after using the bathroom? There are germs everywhere!" At that point, Brad and I both turned to the audience, smiled, and I said, "Now, you just experienced the beginning of a booktalk of *Kissing Doorknobs*, which is about a girl with obsessive-compulsive disorder. Compare Brad's performance to my boring words about the book. Instead of just talking, booktalk."

The following is a selected list of suggested resources on booktalking that may be helpful as you prepare to write and perform booktalks to extreme teens:

Baxter, Kathleen, and Marcia Agness Kochel. 1999. **Gotcha! Nonfiction Booktalks to Get Kids Excited about Reading**. Englewood, CO: Libraries Unlimited. Baxter and Kochel include generic nonfiction topics such as animals, unsolved mysteries, and fascinating people. With a bit of creativity, librarians could use these sample booktalks with extreme teens. For example, the section on unsolved mysteries relates to missing and runaway teens; or it may be useful to promote books about the human body to pregnant and parenting teens. Another noteworthy book by Baxter and Kochel is **Gotcha Again! More Nonfiction Booktalks to Get Kids Excited about Reading** (Libraries Unlimited, 2002).

Bodart, Joni. 2002. **Radical Reads: 101 YA Novels on the Edge**. Lanham, MD: Scarecrow Press. Bodart provides tips for writing booktalks and book reports, information about censorship, and a thorough list of sample books. Each entry includes a list of the subject areas covered, information about the characters, a sample booktalk, major themes and ideas, strengths and risks of the book, reviews, whether the book is an award winner, and ideas for writing book reports. Some of the books that feature extreme teens include *Breathing Underwater* (2001) by Alex Flinn, *Tenderness* (1997) by Robert Cormier, *Like Sisters on the Homefront* (1995) by Rita Williams Garcia, *Holes* (1998) by Louis Sachar, and *The Body of Christopher Creed* (2000) by Carol Plum-Ucci.

Bromann, Jennifer. 2001. **Booktalking That Works**. New York: Neal-Schuman. Bromann presents creative ideas for booktalking, how to write without reading, hooking your audience, practical advice about techniques, preparing to booktalk, and working with schools. There are several examples of booktalks, and some of these titles feature extreme teens, including *Hard Love* (1999) by Ellen Wittlinger, *Kissing the Witch* (1997) by Emily Donoghue, and *Making Up Megaboy* (1998) by Virginia Walter. For additional booktalking advice, see Bromann, **More Booktalking That Works** (Neal-Schuman 2005).

Cox, Ruth E. 2002. **Tantalizing Tidbits for Teens: Quick Booktalks for the Busy High School Media Specialist**. Worthington, OH: Linworth Publishing. This resource includes annual recommended reading lists, information about awards, booktalking techniques, and sample booktalks. Although this book was published for high school media specialists, public librarians will also benefit from using the sample booktalks. Some of the sample booktalks that relate to extreme teens include *Baby Be-Bop* (1975) by Francesca Lia Block, *Smack* (1998) by Melvin Burgess, *Mary Wolf* (1995) by Cynthia D. Grant, *Get It While It's Hot. Or Not* (1996) by Valerie Hobbs, *Monster: A Novel* (1999) by Walter Dean Myers, *Tomorrow Wendy: A Love Story* (1998) by Shelley Stoehr, *Damned Strong Love: The True Story of Willi G. and Stephan K.* (1995) by Lutz Van Dijk, and *When Kambia Elaine Flew in from Neptune* (2000) by Lori Aurelia Williams.

Langemack, Chapple. 2003. **Booktalker's Bible: How to Talk about the Books You Love to Any Audience**. Englewood, CO: Libraries Unlimited. This is a general how-to guide on booktalking. It covers how to find your audience, choose books, build and deliver a booktalk, and evaluate your performance. It includes a chapter on booktalking to children and teens, with special tips on booktalking in schools. Sample booktalks and booklists for a wide variety of audiences are also provided.

Novelist is a very useful database that provides readers' advisory services to library patrons. Many independent, consortium, and state library agencies provide access to *Novelist* and other electronic databases. There are sample booktalks for juvenile and young adult books. In many cases, there is more than one booktalk sample per book, which have been written by librarians throughout the United States. Because of the diversity of booktalkers who have submitted entries, *Novelist* is extremely useful for getting ideas for different ways to booktalk the same title. Also, since it is an online database, librarians have access to sample booktalks of new titles in a relatively short time period. *Novelist* also includes an article by Tom Reynolds titled "Booktalking: Selling Books to Teenagers," and it is useful for those who wish to explore different booktalking techniques.

Extreme Teen Tidbits: Advice about Booktalking

- Provide teens with a list of the books you are going to booktalk, along with the author, call number, and a brief annotation.
- When selecting books to present, keep your audience in mind. Do you know their reading levels?

- If you have only booktalked in classrooms, and you are not accustomed to booktalking in alternative locations such as detention centers and group homes, become as familiar as possible with these new locations before your first visit. Visiting a juvenile detention center for the first time may be daunting. The space where you will be performing may be crowded, open, surrounded by guards, or somewhat less rigid than you had expected. The only way to find out is to visit the location before your first scheduled visit.

- There is no correct answer to the question of when a booktalk should be first written down. What works for me is to simply form booktalks in my head while I am reading the book. If I stumble on a great scene with a lot of blood, or an emotional character who tugs at my heart, or a powerful quotation that makes me stumble, I become inspired. Typically, I can envision an idea from what I have read. I can mold this into a booktalk by picturing myself on stage, in front of an audience of eager extreme teens. I jot down notes when I read the book and form the booktalk in my head, but I do not dwell on useless details. Only what pertains to my performance.

- If you like to use props in your booktalks, and you are visiting a juvenile detention center, make sure beforehand that you will be allowed to bring those props into the building.

Sample Booktalks

The following are sample booktalks of titles specifically about extreme teens. Be forewarned, however, that these booktalks represent my personal style. Once you have performed a number of booktalks, you will establish your own style and methods for delivering an exciting performance. In order to learn about different ways in which these titles can be presented, I urge you to observe other librarians as they booktalk.

If you are planning to perform booktalks to an extreme teen audience, consider the needs of your audience and speak with the person in charge of the group beforehand. It may not be useful to booktalk titles that only deal with nontraditional teens to an extreme teen audience. You may find that it is more beneficial to present different types of books, both fiction and nonfiction. If you are going to work with the same group of teens over a period of time, you may want to consider giving them some type of written survey or talking to them about the types of books that they would be interested in hearing about.

Often, young adult fiction includes characters who may fall into a number of categories of nontraditional teens. You may want to focus on the main character and his or her dilemma, but if you are trying to reach a certain audience, you may choose to concentrate on another scene or character. If one excellent book features many extreme characters, perhaps you could introduce all of them to the audience through booktalking.

For example, **Keesha's House**, a 2004 Michael L. Printz Award Honor Book written by Helen Frost, features six characters who are all nontraditional. If you wanted to focus on gay teens or runaways, you could focus on Harris, but there is also Stephie, who is pregnant, and Dontay, who is in foster care while his parents are in prison. Keesha ran away from home. Carmen is in a juvenile detention center after being arrested for DUI, and Katie struggles with an abusive stepfather. The author describes the characters in verse. So, an easy way to promote the book is to incorporate some readers' theater into your booktalk. Ask for audience members to volunteer after fully explaining that they will need to read out loud. Without this forewarning, you may cause a lot of embarrassment depending on the reading abilities of the teens you are trying to reach. Photocopy pages from the book that focus on different characters, choosing exceptional scenes that give a feel for the book. For example, "Do Not Leave Children Unattended" explains how Harris uses the library to brush his teeth, wash his hair, shave, listen to music, do his homework, and play computer games. Using this scene is an easy way to promote the library, its resources, and to begin a discussion about homelessness.

Booktalks about Delinquency, Incarceration, and Violence

Gantos, Jack. 2002. **Hole in My Life**. New York: Farrar, Straus and Giroux.

2003 Michael L. Printz Award Honor Book

Description: This autobiography details how and why the author lived a life of crime during his late teen years and details his experiences in prison.

(Read from the book) I was nineteen, still stuck in high school, and I wasn't living at home. I had unlimited freedom. No supervision whatsoever. I had spending money. I had a fast car. I had a fake ID. My entire year was a grand balancing act between doing what I wanted and doing

what I should, and being who I was while inventing who I wanted to be: a writer with something important to say. (p. 9)

These are the words of author Jack Gantos. It might sound like he had a great life at the age of nineteen. He had all the freedom in the world. For a little while, anyway.

Eventually, that freedom did a complete turn. Before he knew it, he was in prison. He had agreed to sail a yacht loaded with hashish from the Virgin Islands to New York City. Well, he got caught, and he spent years in prison. This was the worst time of his life, except for one thing. He had lots of time to write. In prison he discovered that writing was a gift for him. It kept him afloat during a hard time in his life.

Read what he has to say about prison, writing, and fulfilling dreams.

Rodriguez, Joseph. 2004. **Juvenile**. New York: Powerhouse Books.

Description: The author, who spent time in prison, explores the lives of young offenders through black and white photography. Most of the photographs feature inmates at the Santa Clara County Juvenile Hall in San Jose, California. Interspersed with information about how these teens ended up in a juvenile detention center are statistics about juvenile crime and insightful quotations from the teens, their family members, and their probation officers. The introduction, written by Nell Bernstein, chronicles the history of juvenile court and focuses on Proposition 21.

(Speaking loudly) JUVENILE!

What are the words that you associate with that word?

Delinquent? Criminal? Perhaps the SLAM (slam your fist on something that won't break) of a cell door shutting. Maybe you hear the sound of guards yelling, or inmates crying. Or stifling their feelings.

(Speaking softly) Silence. Maybe you don't hear anything at all when you think of that word. (Speaking loudly again) JUVENILE.

(Speaking softly again, pacing around the room, watching the audience, making eye contact) Maybe you think about what life is like outside of this place.

Green trees. The shock of cold water when you jump into a lake. The smell of burgers on the grill. Walking on the sidewalk, kicking colorful leaves in October. Watching the snow pile up in the winter as the snowflakes slowly drift toward Earth.

(Normal voice) But maybe you should think about how you are going to survive when you get out of here. Will you have a place to stay? How will you get

a job? Do you have any children you'll need to feed? Parents you'll need to help support?

Joseph Rodriguez knows what you are going through. He's a photographer. He's been where you've been. Literally. Joseph is the author of this book, called **Juvenile**.

That's right (loud voice), JUVENILE. Joseph was at Rikers Island in the 1970s. Why? Well, he could not kick his habit, so he became a dealer. Years later, when his mom was sorting through some stuff, she found letters that Joseph had written while he was at Rikers. Copies of the letters are also in his book.

The rest of the book shows photos of teenagers, just like you, as they experience incarceration. (Hold up the book to the audience, show various photographs, and read the captions. Note that the book does not have page numbers, so you'll need to mark the appropriate pages beforehand.) The book also has photos of teens after they get out of prison, and how they try to cope in the world. Think it is going to be easy?

Consider Charles, who lives in a hotel in San Francisco with his girl, Krea, and Charles Jr. They can't afford day care. Charles has been sending out resumés, but still does not have a job.

There are success stories, too, though. Don't get discouraged. Once you get out of here, you can try to make the best of it. Joseph Rodriguez did.

Vona, Abigail. 1999. **Confessions of a Teenage Delinquent**. Cambridge, MA: Candlewick Press.

Description: The author describes her experiences at Peninsula Village, a treatment facility where she was placed at age fifteen by her father after living a reckless life.

I was one of the fortunate ones. I was selected to move into one of the cabins. It was a luxury compared to what life was like before.

The only drawback to the cabins? Using the outhouses. The stench was incredible. Not only that, but I had to walk from the cabin to the outhouse with a bunch of other girls, who were also going to use the outhouse right before or after I did. Now, that's a little too close for comfort.

And when a group of boys walked past? Well, we all had to duck our heads. We were not allowed to even look at them. The trips to the outhouse were uneventful, unless one of the girls got out of control—you know, beating up a shrink or harassing a gardener.

But still, living in the cabins was better than the alternative—being locked up in a room wearing a nightgown, forced to being restrained at times.

This is the true story of Abby Vona. At age fifteen, her father decides that she is out of control—stealing, drinking, using drugs, and hanging out with older boys—so he decides to take her to camp. Well, camp actually turns out to be a treatment facility. In the beginning, you will probably side with Abby, thinking that her behavior was not that bad and that her father was being ridiculous.

By the end, though, you might realize that Abby had a lot of growing up to do, and that being forced into difficult living arrangements actually saved her life.

A Booktalk about Emancipated Teens

Haddix, Margaret Peterson. 1996. **Don't You Dare Read This, Mrs. Dunphrey**. New York: Simon and Schuster.

Description: In the journal she is keeping for English class, sixteen-year-old Tish chronicles the changes in her life after her parents abandon her and her younger brother.

(Chew gum loudly, talk very rapidly, and sit poised in a chair)

I'm Tish. I'm NOT one of those girls in school who does everything right and brings the teacher an apple. I'm one of the girls with the big hair. You know the type. You know what they say about us. I don't even have to go there. You know what I mean. Everyone thinks that life is so easy for us. We are the popular crowd in school. Nobody messes with us.

(Pause, and talk in normal voice after spitting out gum) Okay, I just pretended to be Tish. Of course there are girls in every school like Tish. You know the type I'm talking about. There are probably some in this room (pause in anticipation of snickering).

Well, Tish THINKS that she's all that. She acts like she's not afraid of any-thing, but she is. See, her parents both left. She's what we call "emancipated"—meaning that she is living on her own. Not by her choice, though—she's pretty much been abandoned.

Sounds great, right? No parents around? Well, it is not that great for Tish. She's trying to raise her younger brother. She has to pay all of the bills. She is broke. She can't even wash her clothes. She can't afford the detergent. She works part-time at Burger Boy, but that's not enough money to pay all of the bills. Tish tells her story in a diary format to her teacher, who promises not to read about her miserable life. But you can.

A Booktalk about a Bisexual Teen

Ryan, Sara. 2001. **Empress of the World**. New York: Viking.

Description: While attending a summer institute, Nic, fifteen, meets another girl named Battle, falls in love with her, and finds the relationship to be difficult and confusing.

I still think about her. After all these years.

Sure, both of our lives have moved on, but those memories keep creeping back. Just when I think that I'm over her, something will take me back to that summer. Perhaps it is a song on the radio. Someone I meet who has similar body language, or resembles her. That was the best summer of my life. I was in school.

Oh, I know what you are thinking, who wants to be in school during the summer? Well, I did not mind, especially on the first day, when we first met.

(Hold up book) This is a love story. There's a triangle involved. Two girls and one boy. It all began one summer. Many of us can remember what it is like to be in love, and worse—or, maybe better, depending on how you look at it—what it is like to miss someone, years later. And knowing that the person you still love is probably with someone else.

Booktalks about Runaway Teens

Davis, Amanda. 2004. **Wonder When You'll Miss Me: A Novel**. New York: Perennial.

Description: After being attacked at a homecoming game, Faith Duckle, sixteen, seeks a new identity and a new home with a traveling circus. This book was awarded the Alex Award in 2004.

I am going to tell you something sad right up front, so just be prepared. I want to give you the bad news first so that you don't think I tricked you into this. The author of this book (show book) is dead.

Sad but true. After she wrote this book, her plane crashed into a mountain in North Carolina. And she wasn't alone. Her parents were with her. She was only thirty-two years old when she died. Now, that might seem old to you, but it's really not. So what is this book about?

Ironically, it is about someone who wants to die. Faith Duckle. After being attacked at a party, she tries to kill herself. Of course this lands her in the loony bin, where she meets all types of people.

When she returns to her school, she can't handle seeing her attackers again. So what does she do? She decides that, indeed, she DOES want to live; just not in that town. So she takes off and joins the circus (pause, since there will probably be laughter).

Okay, you might think it is funny to join the circus, but for Faith it sure beats going to school every day, being surrounded by people who got away with attacking her.

Now, back to the author. Remember, the one who died in the plane crash? She'd probably be glad to know that those of you who may be suffering out there, who have thought about dying, bothered to pick up her book. Perhaps you'll feel more hopeful after reading it, and have more faith in your life.

Flinn, Alex. 2004. **Nothing to Lose**. New York: HarperTempest.

Description: A year after running away with a traveling carnival to escape his unbearable home life, sixteen-year-old Michael returns to Miami, Florida, to find that his mother is going on trial for the murder of his abusive stepfather.

(Pass out copies of the first page, which is a newspaper article with the headline "Jury Selection Begins in Monroe Murder Trial." Give the audience a few moments to look at the article, and depending on the reading abilities of the group, consider reading the article out loud.)

This article says that Michael was missing shortly before the alleged homicide took place. Where do you think he went? Why do you think that he was missing? (Allow audience to respond, and continue the conversation based on their responses.)

All of your answers are interesting, but actually, Michael decides to leave town with a traveling fair. Why? Well, he is in love. Yes, love. Is he in love with someone who operates the ferris wheel? Or the bumper cars, perhaps? It does not really matter.

The important thing is, Michael is in love, and by leaving the town where his mother is being charged with killing her husband, he'll finally have time to think about his life and where it is headed.

A Booktalk about Homeless Teens

Grant, Cynthia D. 1997. **Mary Wolf**. New York: Simon and Schuster.

Description: Mary, sixteen, tries to keep her family together as they aimlessly travel the country after her father's business fails and he starts to change.

How would you like to travel around the country in an RV with your entire family? (Wait for the responses from the audience. Explain to those who like the idea that there is no specific destination and that during the trip they would be forced to spend most of their time with younger siblings, leaving friends behind.)

Mary Wolf is homeless. She lives in an RV with her family, but she has no permanent home. She struggles with this arrangement because her mom has to steal so that the family can eat, her siblings watch television all day, and her father is getting out of control. Mary keeps asking her parents when they'll finally settle down in one spot, but they never have an answer for her. Instead, they keep wandering around the country while Mary's father becomes increasingly violent. Mary decides that she has to protect her family, and she takes it on herself to put an end to her homelessness.

A Booktalk about Pregnant and Parenting Teens

Johnson, Angela. 2003. **The First Part Last**. New York: Simon and Schuster.

2004 Michael L. Printz Award winner

Description: Bobby's carefree teenage life changes forever when he becomes a father and must care for his adored baby daughter, Feather.

You've probably heard that you can't judge a book by its cover. That's a lie.

Lots of times, you can tell just by looking at a book whether it's going to be any good. Why else would publishers spend so much money on designing book covers? So now I'm going to do a little experiment. I'm going to show a few of you a book cover and see how you react. Okay, ready?

(Show the book cover to people who seem very interested as well as those who do not seem to care at all. Chances are, once there is an initial reaction to the cover, other people will lean over and try to see it. Typically, with this cover, showing a handsome teen male holding a small baby wearing pink, you'll hear lots of oohs and aahs from the females in the room. The guys tend to shy away or shrug.)

So what is your reaction? Would you want to read this book based on the cover? (Let them respond.) The guy on the cover is Bobby. On his sixteenth birthday, he finds out that his girlfriend Nia is pregnant. His life changes pretty fast after the baby is born because he has custody of his daughter. Her name is Feather.

So if you liked the cover of this book, you just might like the book. It is a story about a boy who has to grow up too fast. Why? Well, because, sometimes fate gets in the way of plans.

Oh, and before you ask, no, I don't have the telephone number for the guy on the cover. His name is not Bobby. He is just a model for the cover.

Again, remember that everyone needs to develop their own style of booktalking. What works for some librarians may not be exciting enough for another booktalking performer. The reaction that you get from teens when you perform booktalks should also help you decide how to shape your future booktalks. If the reaction was positive, you probably won them over and should continue with the same style. If not, keep trying. No matter what, be yourself and enjoy what you are doing, because if you do not like performing as a booktalker, extreme teens will most likely see right through you, and you will be presenting a poor image of the library.

CONCLUSION

You can boast that you have the best public library in the world, but unless the public knows about it and uses your services, you might as well turn the library into a computer museum with old Commodore 64s sitting around. Teens, as a group, need librarians who understand them. You need to promote the library to attract teenagers in general, and getting extreme teens to the library may be even more challenging. Make sure that the library is a welcoming place from the moment the library patron steps foot on library property. If staff members are helpful and friendly, extreme teens will probably return and tell their friends to visit as well. Teens who have a bad experience may do errands instead of visiting the library, such as getting a haircut. They may never return to the library, and they may convince their friends not to even bother. Remember that library directors can help to shape services to extreme teens, but they need to know what you have accomplished in your efforts to serve these deserving teens.

WORKS CITED

Anderson, Sheila B. 2005. "Flashback to Fantasyland: It's Off to Work We Go." **Young Adult Library Services** (Winter): 3.

Thompson, Stephanie. 2000. "Targeting Teens Means Building Buzz." **Advertising Age** 71, no. 13 (March 27): 26.

FOR FURTHER READING

Ammon, Bette, and Gale W. Sherman. 1998. **More Rip-Roaring Reads for Reluctant Teen Readers**. Westport, CT: Libraries Unlimited.

Anderson, Sheila B., ed. 2004. **Serving Older Teens**. Westport, CT: Libraries Unlimited.

Anderson, Sheila B., and John P. Bradford. 2001. "Frances Henne/YALSA/VOYA Research Grant Results: State-Level Commitment to Public Library Services to Young Adults." **Journal of Youth Services in Libraries** 14, no. 3 (Spring): 23–27.

Anderson, Sheila B., and Kristine Mahood. 2001. "The Inner Game of Booktalking." *Voice of Youth Advocates* 24, no. 4 (June): 107.

Braun, Linda W. 2003. **Hooking Teens with the Net**. New York: Neal-Schuman.

———. 2003. **Technically Involved: Technology-Based Youth Participation Activities for Your Library**. Chicago: American Library Association.

Cormier, Robert. 1991. **We All Fall Down**. New York: Delacorte.

Cox, Ruth E. 2002. **Tantalizing Tidbits for Teens: Quick Booktalks for the Busy High School Library Media Specialist**. Worthington, OH: Linworth.

De Vos, Gail. 2003. **Storytelling for Young Adults: A Guide to Tales for Teens**. 2nd ed. Westport, CT: Librares Unlimited.

Edwards, Kirsten. 2002. **Teen Library Events: A Month-by-Month Guide**. Westport, CT: Greenwood Press.

Edwards, Margaret. 1969. **The Fair Garden and the Swarm of Beasts: The Library and the Young Adult**. New York: Hawthorn Books.

Frost, Helen. 2003. **Keesha's House**. New York: Farrar, Straus and Giroux.

Herald, Diana. 1995. "Booktalking to a Captive Audience." *School Library Journal* 41 (May): 35–36.

Hesser, Terry Spencer. 1998. **Kissing Doorknobs**. New York: Delacorte.

Honnold, RoseMary. 2003. **101+ Teen Programs That Work**. New York: Neal-Schuman.

Jones, Patrick. 2002. **New Directions for Library Services to Young Adults**. Chicago, IL: American Library Association.

Jones, Patrick, Michele Gorman, and Tricia Suellentrop. 2004. **Connecting Young Adults and Libraries: A How-To-Do-It Manual**. 3rd ed. New York: Neal-Schuman.

Jones, Patrick, and Joel Shoemaker. 2001. **Do It Right! Best Practices for Serving Young Adults in School and Public Libraries**. New York: Neal-Schuman.

Littlejohn, Carol, and Cathlyn Thomas. 2001. **Keep Talking That Book! Booktalks to Promote Reading Grades 2–12**. Worthington, OH: Linworth.

Nichols, C. Allen, ed. 2004. **Thinking Outside the Book: Alternatives for Today's Teen Library Collections**. Westport, CT: Libraries Unlimited.

Nichols, C. Allen, and Mary Anne Nichols. 1998. **Young Adults and Public Libraries: A Handbook of Materials and Services**. Westport, CT: Greenwood Press.

O'Dell, Katie. 2002. **Library Materials and Services for Teen Girls**. Westport, CT: Libraries Unlimited.

Osborne, Robin, and Carla D. Hayden. 2004. **From Outreach to Equity: Innova-**

tive **Models of Library Policy and Practice**. Chicago, IL: American Library Association.

Schall, Lucy. 2001. **Booktalks Plus : Motivating Teens to Read**. Westport, CT: Libraries Unlimited.

Vaillancourt, Renee J. 2000. **Bare Bones Young Adult Services: Tips for Public Library Generalists**. Chicago, IL: American Library Association.

Walter, Virginia A., and Elaine Meyers. 2003. **Teens and Libraries: Getting It Right**. Chicago, IL: American Library Association.

Woodward, Jeanette. 2004. **Creating the Customer-Driven Library**. Chicago, IL: American Library Association.

CONCLUSION

> By his easy laugh, the idea that he is only a little more than a
> half-year removed from emergency brain surgery seems al-
> most impossible. Severe headaches just last year turned up
> bleeding inside his brain. He and his family prepared for the
> worst and happily accepted the best when he came through
> surgery with no ill effects.
> —Suzanne Marino, "A Magical Pair," **Current of EHT**
> (February 11, 2004): 8

Who is this extreme teen, a survivor of cancer and bleeding in his brain?
His name is Chad Juros, a magician otherwise know as Chadakazam. He
was diagnosed with leukemia at age three and spent seventeen months
at the Children's Hospital of Philadelphia. His father, who practiced
magic as a hobby, began teaching him a different magic trick each week
while Chadakazam was in the hospital. He spent hours perfecting his
tricks with his father, who passed away from cancer in 2000. Now,
Chadakazam, who was a high school sophomore in 2004, has taken his
magic show on the road to places like Disney World, the White House for
the annual Easter Egg Roll, and as a part of the First Night celebration on
New Year's Eve at the Dover Public Library in 2004.

Does Chadakazam, or someone like him, exist in your community? In addition to focusing your thoughts on the types of extreme teens who have been the subject of this book, think about your own community and other types of teens who experience nontraditional situations. Perhaps you need to reach out to teens who fall outside the mainstream because of medical conditions, or to teens with learning disabilities or physical challenges. Maybe the teens in your community are nontraditional because they live in a rural setting and are far removed from the library. The possibilities are many. How can you better serve these teens so that they will grow into adults who respect, support, and admire libraries and librarians?

The mission statements of many public libraries include the goals of reaching a diverse population through programs, services, and collections. Extreme teens naturally fit under this umbrella of a specialized service population. Adapting to a changing community is not a new experience for most public library employees. Historically, the demographics of the United States have continued to change, which, in turn, will continue to be a factor for libraries in the future. Extreme teens need special services because of their unique circumstances. Reaching out to them and providing them with stellar library services is the first step in creating a community of library users.

My community in Dover, Delaware, serves a unique population. Often, I peek out my bedroom window and see a familiar sight in the darkness. Heading down the street, past my backyard, are the bright purple neon lights that decorate a small black Amish buggy, led by horsepower. About five minutes earlier, I was forwarned of its arrival by loud, thudding music. Amish teenagers frequently pass by the perimeters of my neighborhood, and they announce their existence like any other teenager might: by expressing themselves with loud music or bold colors that cannot be missed. Amish teenagers, at age sixteen, enter a period of their lives in which they are allowed to have the same freedoms as "English" teenagers. During this time, they can decide to enter mainstream society or return to their familiar Amish ways. They make choices that will affect the rest of their lives. Extreme teens can have the same choices, and the library community can be a part of helping teens make these choices.

As librarians serving teens, you are in a unique position to help those who may not fit into the mainstream. Devise a plan to reach them, promote library resources, and help them reach their potential. Hire them to work at the library, train them as volunteers, and promote librarianship as a career so that the profession becomes even more diverse. Perhaps these extreme teens will soon be your colleagues at the library, helping other extreme teens to use the library and improve their lives.

INDEX

ABA Center on Children and the Law, 36

Aborlleile, Alex, 27–28

abortion, 6, 38

academic libraries, xxi

Acting (Winston), 119

"Addressing the Needs of Homeless Students" (Holloway), 30

administrative support, 146–147

adolescence, stages of, 63–65

Alabama, marriage laws in, 85

Allen Guttnacher Institute, 44–45

Alma Mater (Brown), 128

Always My Child (Jennings and Shapiro), 48

American Homelessness, A Reference Handbook (Hombs), 30

American Homeschool Association, 15

Anderson, Sheila B., 81

And What about College? (Cohen), 115

Annie on My Mind (Garden), 99

Arnold, Mary, 76

arrests, statistics on, 8

Assault on Gay America (video), 131

Association of Special and Cooperative Library Agencies, 61

Assumptions, about extreme teens, 55–56; counterproductive, xix; of mainstream young adult services, xx

at-risk youth, defined, xviii

audiobooks, 104

Austin, Susan, xviii

Baldwin, James, 99

Battle of Jericho (Draper), 106

Beet Fields (Paulsen), 112

Before Stonewall (Bullough), 129

Beginner's Luck (Pederson), 109

Being with Henry (Brooks), 111

Bermudez Triangle (Johnson), 128

"Beyond Picket Fences" (Linville), 48

bilingual students, xviii. *See also* ESL
  teens
Bi Lives (Orndorff), 130
Birkerts, Stephen, 20
birth rates, adolescent, 6
bisexual teens. *See* gay, lesbian, bisex-
  ual, transgender, and questioning
  (GLBTQ) teens
*Bisexual Women in the Twenty-first Cen-
  tury* (Atkins), 47, 130
Blue Mirror, The (Koja), 111–112
board games, 121
Body Alchemy (Cameron), 47
Body of Christopher Creed (Plum-Ucci),
  112
Book Bridges for ESL Students (Reid), 25
"Book Group Behind Bars, The" (Ang-
  ier and O'Dell), 34
booklists, 103
Book of Gay Lists (Rutlegde), 130
Book of Hard Things, The (Halpern), 118
"Books Behind Bars" (Madenski), 34
books on tape, 104
Booktalker's Bible (Langemack), 150
Booktalking That Works (Bromann),
  149
booktalks, 147–148; learning to give,
  148–151; sample, 151–159
Borrowed Light (Feinberg), 118
Boxer, The (Karr), 105
Boy Meets Boy (Levithan), 127
Bradford, John P., 84
Breakable Vow, The (Clarke), 111
Breakout (Fleischman), 110
Breathing Underwater (Flinn), 105
Bringing Up the Bones (Zeises), 125
Brown, Fleda, 43
*Building an ESL Collection for Young
  Adults* (McCaffery), 25
"Bumper Sticker Curriculum, The"
  (Norton-Meier), 22
Bureau of Justice Assistance, 36
Burgess, Melvin, 27

Came, Barry, 29
Can't Get There from Here (Strasser),
  112
Catcher in the Rye, The (Salinger), 99
Catch Me If You Can (Abagnale and
  Redding), 9
Center for the Study of Rural Librari-
  anship, 61
Century of Juvenile Justice (Rosenheim),
  35
Chambers, Aidan, 99
Chicago Blues (Deaver), 84
Chicken Soup for the Prisoner's Soul
  (Canfield), 107
children, of teens, 8. *See also* parenting
  teens
Chill Wind (McDonald), 119
Chipper (Collier), 111
Clay's Way (Mastbaum), 127
Close-Up (Dudevszky), 109
Coal Miner's Bride, A (Bartoletti), 115
cohabitating teens, 39–40, 84–86. *See
  also* married teens
collection development, 95–96; policies for, 79, 96–97; resources for,
  105–134. *See also* library collections
Come Clean (Herman), 125
community, gathering information
  about local, 4–5
computer access, 104
computer hacking, 32–33
computer software, 104–105
conferences, 61–62
Confessions of a Teenage Delinquent
  (Vona), 154–155
confidentiality issues, 65–66
Contents Under Pressure (Zeises), 119
Cosmos Coyote and William the Nice
  (Heynen), 106
Crazy Horse Electric Game (Crutcher),
  99
crime, 32–37
Crime and Criminals (Roleff), 107

Criminological Theory, 36
Crossing into America (Mendoza and Shankar), 115–116
"Crossing Two Bridges" (Sanchez), 48
Crowe, Cameron, 9
Crutcher, Chris, 99
Cuba 15 (Osa), 116
Cybrary Criminal Justice Directory, 36

Dance for Three (Plummer), 119
Dance on My Grave (Chambers), 99
Dancing Naked (Hrdlitschka), 118
Daycare and Diplomas (South Vista Education Center), 121
Deaver, Julie Reece, 84
delinquent teens, 32–37; booktalks about, 152–155; DVDs and videos about, 108; fiction about, 105–106; nonfiction about, 107; organizations about, 108–109; serving, 75–83
demographics, of extreme teens, 4–5; local, xvii–xix
Department of Children and Families (DFC), 28
Dewey Decimal System, 102
Diamond Dogs (Watt), 106
Dirt on Sex, The (Lookadoo), 126
diversity, sensitivity to, xix
Do I Have a Daddy? (Hurley), 120
Doing It (Burgess), 124
Doll Baby (Bunting), 118
Donorboy (Halpin), 129
Don't Think Twice (Pennebaker), 119
Don't You Dare Read This, Mrs. Dunphrey (Haddix), 155–156
Double Life of Zoe Flynn (Carey), 111
Down and Out, on the Road (Kusmer), 30
Dreamland (Dessen), 106
Drexler, Melissa, 43
dropouts, xviii, 17–19; fiction about, 109; nonfiction for, 101; serving, 67–68; statistics on, 7–8

dual-enrollment students, 16–17, 66–67, 101
DVDs, 103; about delinquency, incarceration, and violence, 108; about GLBTQ teens, 131–132
Dykes and Sundry Other Carbon-based Life Forms to Watch Out For (Bechdel), 128

educational situations, 11–25; dropouts, 17–19; dual enrollment, 16–17; English as Second Language (ESL), 22–25; homeschooling, 13–16; literacy and reluctant readers, 20–22; unschooling, 11–13
Eight Seconds (Ferris), 127
emancipated teens, xx, 37–39; booktalks about, 155–156; fiction about, 109; nonfiction about, 101, 109; serving, 83–84
empathy, power of, 2
Empress of the World (Ryan), 127, 156
Encyclopedia of Homelessness (Levinson), 30
Encyclopedia of Juvenile Justice (McShane), 35
English as Second Language (ESL). *See* ESL teens
ESL Beginner (Boguchwal), 116
ESL teens, 22–25; fiction about, 115–116; nonfiction about, 116–117; online resources for, 117–118; organizations for, 117–118; serving, 70–72
Esperanza Rising (Ryan), 116
Ethics of Abortion (Hurley), 120
Everything Father-to-Be Book (Nelson), 121
Everything Homeschooling Book, The (Lindsenbach), 15
Everything You Need to Know if You and Your Parents Are New Americans (Santos), 116–117

Exploding the Myths (Aronson), 21
extreme teens, assumptions about, 55–
56; books about, 9; defined, xviii–
xix; demographics of, 4–5; diversity
of, 3–4; information-seeking by, xxi;
involving, in library programming,
56; learning from, 143–144; librarians who were, 10; music about, 10;
networking with, 144–146; reasons
to serve, xxi; special considerations
in serving, 65–66; statistics about, 5–
11; subgroups of, xvii–xix. *See also*
specific types

Faith Wish (Bechard), 118
Families Like Mine (Garner), 131
Famous Crimes of the 20th Century
(Marzilli), 107
Fast Girls (White), 42
fathers, teen, 86–87
Feeling Sorry for Celia (Moriarty), 112
Fiction, about delinquency, 105–106;
benchmark novels, 99; about
dropouts, 109; about emancipated
teens, 109; about ESL and immigrant
teens, 115–116; about foster care, 109–
110; about GLBTQ teens, 126–129;
about homelessness, 111–112; about
incarceration, 105; in library collections, 98–100; about married teens,
111; about pregnant and parenting
teens, 118–119; realistic, 98; about
runaways, 112–113; about sexuality,
124–125; about violence, 105–106
Finding H. F. (Watts), 129
Fires in the Bathroom (Cushman), 24
First Crossing (Gallo), 115
First Part Last, The (Johnson), 158–159
Flight to Freedom (Veciana-Suarez), 116
Forbes, Leslie, 29
Foreman, Judy, 39
foster care, 28, 30–32; fiction about,
109–110; online resources about,

110–111; statistics on, 9; videos
about, 110
"Foster-Care Children Are Poorly Educated" (Blair), 31
Foster Care Odyssey (Cameron), 31
free-choice learning, 12. *See also* unschooling
funding cuts, to public libraries, xvii–
xvii

Gang Crime Prevention Center, 36
Garden, Nancy, 99
Garrison, Jessica, 13
Gay and Lesbian Fiction for Young
Adults (Cart), 47
Gay, Lesbian, Bisexual and Transgen-
dered (GLBT) Round Table, 61
gay, lesbian, bisexual, transgender,
and questioning (GLBTQ) teens, 45–
48; booktalks about, 156; fiction
about, 126–129; homeless, 29; mar-
riage and, 85–86; nonfiction for, 102,
129–131; resources for, 133–135;
serving, 89–90; suicide and, 56;
videos about, 131–132
Gay Pride (Mann), 130
Geography Club (Hartinger), 127
Georgia, marriage laws in, 85
Girl2Girl (Rashid), 131
Girls in Trouble (Leavitt), 118–119
Give a Boy a Gun (Strasser), 106
Giver, The (Lowry), 48
GLBTQ (Huegel), 129
Goldberg, Elliot, 1
Goldberg, Whoopi, 9
Gotcha! Nonfiction Booktalks to Get Kids
Excited about Reading (Baxter and
Kochel), 149
Graduation for All (Lehr, Clapper, and
Thurlow), 19
Grant, Cynthia D., 27
Gravel Queen (Benduhn), 129
Great Depression, 26

Gross, Melissa, 86
Grossberg, Amy, 43
Growing Up Fast (Lipper), 44
Growing Up Gay in America (Rich), 130
Guerilla Learning (Llewellyn and Silver), 13
Guiden, Mary, 43

Haddix, Margaret Peterson, 37
Handbook for Boys (Myers), 106
Hanging on to Max (Bechard), 118
Harmful to Minors (Levine), 42
Harrington-Leuker, Donna, 21
Head, Ann, 39, 99
health issues, 38–39
Hearing All the Voices (Darby and Pryne), 24
high school dropouts, xviii, 17–19; fiction about, 109; nonfiction for, 101; serving, 67–68; statistics on, 7–8
Hine, Thomas, 32
Hinton, S. E., 27, 99
Hold Them in Your Heart (Mundowney), 35
Hole in My Life (Gantos), 152–154
Holes (Sachar), 9
Holly's Secret (Garden), 129
Homeless (Peterson), 113
homeless teens, 26–30; booktalks about, 158; fiction about, 111–112; nonfiction about, 113; serving, 73–75; videos about, 114
homeschoolers, 13–16, 66; nonfiction for, 101, 114–115
Home School, High School, and Beyond (Adams-Gordon), 114–115
Homeschooling (Cohen), 14
Homeschool Support Network, 15
House between Homes, A (Libal), 31
How I Learned to Snap (Read), 130
How It Feels to Have a Gay or Lesbian Parent (Snow), 131
Howser, Doogie, 9

If Beale Could Talk (Baldwin), 99
"Imagine" (Anderson), 81
Imani All Mine (Porter), 119
Immigrant Politics and the Public Library (Luevano-Molina), 24–25
immigrant teens, 22–25; fiction about, 115–116; nonfiction about, 116–117; online resources for, 117–118; organizations for, 117–118; serving, 70–72
Immigration (Hay), 116
incarceration, 32–37, 75–83; DVDs and videos about, 108; fiction about, 105; nonfiction about, 107; organizations about, 108–109
independent teens, 37–39. *See also* emancipated teens
Internet for Educators and Homeschoolers (Jones), 15
infanticide, 43
information, public libraries as source of, xxi
in-house training, 59–60
International Reading Association, 20–21
Internet, reliance on, xx
Internet crime, 32–33
In the Mix (video), 108
Invisible Minority, The (Latham), 48
Invisible Revolution (video), 108
Irons, Paulette, 43
Issues in Immigration (Currie), 116
I Won't Read and You Can't Make Me (Reynolds), 22

Jehovah's Witnesses, 38
Juros, Chad, 163–164
juvenile arrests, statistics on, 8
Juvenile Crime (Ferro), 34
juvenile delinquents, 32–37; fiction about, 105–106; serving, 75–83
Juvenile Justice Bulletin (Butts and Buck), 34
Juvenile Justice Evaluation Center, 36

King, Alex, 33
King, Derek, 33
King (Berger), 111
Kissing Kate (Myracle), 128
Krashen, Stephen, 20

Last Chance Texaco (Hartinger), 110
Leave Myself Behind (Yates), 128
Leave No Child Behind, 21
Legare, Marion, 29
lesbian teens. *See* gay, lesbian, bisexual, transgender, and questioning teens (GLBTQ)
Lessons without Limit (Falk and Dierking), 12
Letting Go of Bobby James (Hobbs), 111
librarians, who were extreme teens, 10
libraries, as important source of information, xx
library atmosphere, 142–143
library collections; fiction in, 98–100; keeping current, 97–98; nonfiction in, 101–102; non-print resources in, 103–105; weeding, 97–98. *See also* collection development
library conferences, 61–62
library directors, 146–147
library organizations, 60–61
library services, geared to extreme teens, xx; promoting, 137–143
"Library Services to Pregnant Teens" (Gross), 44
Library Services to Spanish Speaking Patrons (Moller), 25
library staff, assumptions made by, about extreme teens, 55–56; choosing, to visit detention centers, 80–82; selection of, 58–59; teaching, to empathize with teens, 2–3; training, 59–62
Library Standards for Juvenile Correction Facilities (Association for Specialized and Cooperative Library Agencies), 34
Lipstick (video), 132
literacy, 20–22, 68–69
Literacy and Bilingualism (Brisk and Harrington), 24
"Literacy, Literature, and Diversity" (Hinton and Berry), 24
literature, benchmark novels, 99; quotations from, 100
Living at the Edge of the World (Bolnick and Pastor), 113
living situations, 25–40; cohabitating teens, 39–40; emancipated teens, 37–39; foster care, 30–32; homeless teens, 26–30; incarceration, 32–37; married teens, 39–40; runaways, 26–30
Love Among the Ruins (Clark), 112
Love and Sex (Cart), 124
Lovely Bones, The (Sebold), 106
Lowry, Lois, 48
Lucky (De Oliveira), 127
Lucy Peale (Rodowsky), 26–27
Luna (Peters), 129
Lyman, Isabel, 13

magazines, 103
Mahalia (Horniman), 118
Make Lemonade (Wolff), 99
"Making a Difference" (Herald), 35
Marino, Suzanne, 163
marriage laws, 85–86
married teens, 39–40; fiction about, 111; nonfiction for, 101; serving, 84–86
Maryland, marriage laws in, 85
Mary Wolf (Grant), 27, 158
McCann, Richard A., xviii
media, teens represented in, 33–34
medical issues, 38–39
Metes and Bounds (Quinn), 128
Minner, Ruth Ann, xvii–xviii

Molinder, Ilene, 41
Monster in Me, The (Harris), 110
Monster (Myers), 77–78
"More of Those in Foster Care Are
    Teenagers" (Kaufman), 31
*More Rip-Roaring Readers for Reluctant
    Readers* (Bette and Sherman), 21
Mr. and Mrs. Bo Jo Jones (Head), 39,
    99
Multicultural Projects Index (Pilger), 25
music, about extreme teens, 10
Myers, Walter Dean, 76, 77–78, 106
*My Friend Is Struggling With—Un-
    planned Pregnancy* (McDowell), 120
My Heartbeat (Freymann-Weyr), 127

National Alliance for Safe Schools, 36
National Campaign Against Youth Vi-
    olence Headquarters, 36–37
National Campaign to Prevent Teen
    Pregnancy, 45
National Center for Home Education,
    15
National Crime Prevention Council,
    37
National Criminal Justice Reference
    Service, 37
National Endowment for the Arts
    (NEA), 20
National Gang Crime Research Cen-
    ter, 37
National Home Education Research
    Institute, 16
National Organization of Adolescent
    Pregnancy, Parenting, and Preven-
    tion, 45
National School Safety Center, 37
needs, determining, 57
networking, 62–63; in extreme teen
    community, 144–146
New Gay Teenager, The (Savin-
    Williams), 48
Newly Wed (Krulik), 111

No Home of Your Own (video), 114
Nonfiction; about delinquency, 107;
    about emancipated teens, 109; about
    ESL and immigrant teens, 116–117;
    about GLBTQ teens, 129–131; about
    homelessness, 113; about home-
    schooling, 114–115; about incarcera-
    tion, 107; in library collections, 101–
    102; about pregnant and parenting
    teens, 119–121; about runaways,
    113; about sexuality, 125; about vio-
    lence, 107
non-print resources, 103–105
North (Napoli), 112
Nothing to Lose (Flinn), 157
Not Me, Not Mine (video), 110
Not Our Kind of Girl (Kaplan), 44
Not the Only One (Summer), 126
Novelist, 150
novels, benchmark, 99
Nurturing Your Newborn (Lindsay), 120

Once a Criminal Always a Criminal
    (video), 108
One Night (Wild), 119
*One of Those Hideous Books Where the
    Mother Dies* (Sones), 129
online resources, 103–104; about ESL
    and immigrant teens, 117–118;
    about foster care, 110–111; for
    GLBTQ teens, 132–134; about home-
    lessness, 113–114; for pregnant and
    parenting teens, 121–124; about run-
    aways, 113–114; about sexuality,
    125–126
On Their Own (Shirk, Stangler, and
    Carter), 31
On the Run (Coleman), 106
Organizations; about delinquency,
    incarceration, and violence, 108–109;
    about ESL and immigrant teens,
    117–118; about foster care, 110–111;
    for GLBTQ teens, 132–134; about

homelessness, 113–114; for pregnant
and parenting teens, 121–124; about
runaways, 113–114; about sexuality,
125–126
Orphans of the Living (Toth), 32
Our Mom's a Dyke (video), 132
Our Trans Children (Zavier, Sharp and
Boenke), 131
outreach programs, to incarcerated
teens, 79–82
Outreach to Teens with Special Needs
Committee, xviii, 60–61
Outsiders, The (Hinton), 27

Pages for You (Brownrigg), 128
pamphlets, 103
parenting teens, 43–45; booktalks
about, 158–159; fiction about, 118–
119; nonfiction for, 101, 119–121; organizations for, 121–124; serving,
86–88; statistics on, 8
Paulsen, Gary, 9
Pebble in a Pool (Taylor), 128
Perfect Family (Oughton), 119
Peterson, Brian, 43
Pictures of Hollis Woods (Giff), 110
Plain Truth (Picoult), 119
Playing without the Ball (Wallace), 109
Plunking Reggie Jackson (Bennett), 118
policy issues, 65–66
Pregnant! (Halelr), 120
pregnant teens, 43–45, xix; booktalks
about, 158–159; fiction about, 118–
119; nonfiction about, 101, 119–121;
organizations for, 121–124; serving,
86–88; statistics, 6
Prep (Coburn), 105–106
privacy issues, 65–66
programs, for extreme teens, 56–58;
planning, 5; promotion of, 139–142
promotion, assessment, 138–139;
through atmosphere, 142–143;

through booktalks, 147–159; of library services, 137–142; of programs, 139–142
psychology, adolescent, 63–65
*Public Assault on America's Children,
The* (Polakow), 35
public libraries, as sources of information, xxi; state aid to, xvii–xvii
"Public Libraries and People in Jail"
(McCook), 35

Quinceañera Means Sweet 15 (Chambers), 115

Radical Reads (Bodart), 149
Rainbow Boys (Sanchez), 127
*Reaching Out to Lesbian, Gay, and Bisex-
ual Youth* (video), 132
"Reaching Out to Young Adults in
Jail" (Jones), 35
Reaching Reluctant Young Adult Readers
(Sullivan), 22
reading materials, support for all
types of, 68–69
Reading Rules! Motivating Teens to Read
(Knowles and Smith), 22
realistic fiction, 98
Real-Life Homeschooling (Barfield), 115
Rebman, Renee C., 27
Reckoning with Homelessness (Hopper),
30
recorded books, 104
Redhanded (Cadnum), 105
Reed, Shannon, 89
Refugees (Stine), 116
reluctant readers, 20–22, 68–69
resources, about delinquency, 34–37;
on booktalks, 149–151; on dropouts,
19; about ESL and immigrant teens,
24–25; about foster care, 31–32;
about GLBTQ teens, 47–48, 90;
about homelessness, 30; home-

schooling, 14–16; about literacy and reluctant readers, 21–22; about runaways, 30; about sexuality, 42; on teen pregnancy and parenting, 44–45; about unschooling, 12–13. *See also* online resources

Revolutionary Voices (Sonnie), 130

Reynolds, Marilyn, 99

"Rights of Passage" (Daniel and McEntire), 47

Rodowssky, Colby, 26–27

Rumble Fish (Hinton), 99

Runaway Kids and Teenage Prostitution (Barri), 30

runaways, 26–30; booktalks about, 156–157; fiction about, 112–113; nonfiction about, 113; serving, 73–75

Runaway Teens (Rebman), 113

Salinger, J. D., 99

Salzman, Mark, 32, 36

same-sex parents, 129

Say That to My Face (Prete), 109

school libraries, xxi

School of Beauty and Charm (Whelan), 112–113

Scout's Honor (video), 132

Second Choices (Brinkerhoff), 118

Second Summer of the Sisterhood (Brashares), 124

Serving Homeschooled Teens and Their Parents (Lerch and Welch), 15

Serving the Underserved (SUS) training program, 59–60

Sex (Cann), 125

Sex Explained (Clausener-Petit), 125

"Sex" (Farrell), 42

Sex Lives of Teenagers, The (Ponton), 42

Sex, Puberty, and All That Stuff (Bailey), 125

sexual activity, 40–42

Sexual Century, The (Hickman), 42

sexual identity, 88–90

sexuality, 88–89; fiction about, 124–125; nonfiction about, 102, 125; organizations about, 125–126

Shacked Up (Cann), 109

Shadow of a Doubt (Rottman), 112

Shelterbelt (Baur), 118

Shooter (Myers), 106

Shooting Monarchs (Halliday), 109

Simple Gift, The (Herrick), 112

Sisterhood of the Traveling Pants (Brashares), 124

Slut! Growing Up Female with a Bad Reputation (Tanenbaum), 42

Smack (Burgess), 27

Snowfish (Rapp), 112

software, 104–105

So Hard to Say (Sanchez), 128

Someone There for Me (Fisher), 31

Some Place to Call Home (video), 110

Sons Talk about Their Gay Fathers (Gottlieb), 132

special libraries, xxi

special programs, for extreme teens, 56–58

Spellbound (McDonald), 109

staff selection, 58–59

staff training, 59–60

statistics, 5–11; on abortion, 6; on dropouts, 7–8; on foster care, 9; on juvenile arrests, 8; on teen mothers, 8; on teen pregnancy, 6

Step from Heaven, A (Na), 116

stereotyping, 3

Stewart, Shane, 27

Stuart, Elaine, xvii

Subcommittee on Library Services to the Poor and Homeless, 61

Success without College (Lee), 18

Summer They Came, The (Storandt), 128

Surpassing the Love of Men (Faderman), 131

surveys, of teens, 4–5
Swimming to America (Mead), 115

Taking Responsibility (Lange), 125
Talk (Koja), 127
Tantalizing Tidbits for Teens (Cox), 150
Teaching Sex (Moran), 42
Teenagers, empathizing with, 2–3; information-seeking by, xxi; stereotyping, 3; surveys of, 4–5
teen fathers, 86–87. *See also* parenting teens
Teen Fathers (Endersbe), 120
Teen Fathers Today (Gottfried), 120
Teen Files (video), 108
teen mothers. *See* parenting teens
teen pregnancy. *See* pregnant teens
Teen Pregnancy and Parenting (Cothran), 119–120
teen psychology, 63–65
Teens and Gay Issues (Marcovitz and Gallup), 130
Teens in Turmoil (Maxym and York), 35
teen volunteers, 143–144
Ten Miles from Winnemucca (Wyss), 113
Things Change (Jones), 106
This Book Is about Sex (Shaw), 125
throwaways, 29. *See also* runaways
To Be a Boy, To Be a Reader (Brozo), 22
Too Soon for Jeff (Reynolds), 99
Torch Red (Carlson), 124
Touching Spirit Bear (Mikaelsen), 106
Tough on Crime, Tough on Our Kind (video), 108
training, 59–62
transgender teens. *See* gay, lesbian, bisexual, transgender, and questioning teens (GLBTQ)
Trial (Kuklin), 107
True Notebooks (Salzman), 32, 36
True Test for Skye, A (Woodson), 110
Twelve (McDonell), 109

Underground Guide to Teenage Sexuality (Basso), 125
underserved populations, xviii
Understanding Dropouts (National Research Council), 19
Unexpected Development (Perez), 124
unschooling, 11–13
Urban Library Council, 61
U.S. Department of Justice, 36

Vacca, Richard T., 21
V Club, The (Brian), 124
Vernon God Little (Pierre), 106
videos, 103; about delinquency, incarceration, and violence, 108; about foster care, 110; about GLBTQ teens, 131–32; about homelessness, 114
violence, 32–37; DVDs and videos about, 108; nonfiction about, 107; organizations about, 108–109
Violence in Our Schools (Orr), 107
Vogt, MaryEllen, 20

Walking on Air (Easton), 111
Walking on Water (Jensen), 13
Walk to Remember, A (Sparks), 9, 111
Web sites, 104. *See also* online resources
weeding, 97–98
We're Not Monsters (Weill), 107
What Adolescents Deserve (Irvin and Rycik), 22
What Smart Teenagers Know . . about Dating, Relationships, and Sex (Hatchell), 125
Where the Heart Is (Letts), 9
White Horse, The (Grant), 27
Will the Dollars Stretch? (Pollock), 121
Wolff, Virginia Euwer, 99
Wonder When You'll Miss Me (Davis), 156–157

YALSA. *See* Young Adult Library Services Association

Year of Ice (Malloy), 127

You Look Too Young to Be a Mom (Davis), 43, 120

Young Adult Library Services Association (YALSA), 61, xviii

"Young Adult Sexuality Research" (MacRae), 42

Your Newborn (Natterson), 120

Youth on Trial (Grisso and Schwartz), 35

Zach at Risk (Shepherd), 129

About the Author

SHEILA B. ANDERSON has worked for public libraries in North Carolina, Indiana, and Delaware and is the editor of *Serving Older Teens* (Libraries Unlimited, 2004). She was appointed to the ALA Children's Book Council (CBC) Joint Committee in 2004 and was elected as an ALA Councilor-at-Large in 2003. She has served on the YALSA Board of Directors, the Selected DVDs and Videos for Young Adults Committee, the Selected Audiobooks Committee, the Professional Development Committee, and the Best of the Best Books for Young Adults Preconference Committee. She maintains a Web site at www.sheilabanderson.com.